FORTRESS • 71

THE WALLS OF ROME

NIC FIELDS

ILLUSTRATED BY PETER DENNIS

Series editors Marcus Cowper and Nikolai Bogdanovic

First published in Great Britain in 2008 by Osprey Publishing,
Midland House, West Way, Botley, Oxford OX2 0PH, United Kingdom
443 Park Avenue South, New York, NY 10016, USA
Email: info@ospreypublishing.com

A CIP catalogue record for this book is available from the British Library.

ISBN 978 184603 198 4

Editorial by Ilios Publishing, Oxford, UK (www.iliospublishing.com)
Page layout by Ken Vail Graphic Design, Cambridge, UK (kvgd.com)
Cartography by The Map Studio, Romsey, UK
Typeset in Sabon and Myriad Pro
Index by Alan Thatcher
Originated by United Graphic Pte Ltd, Singapore
Printed and bound in China through Bookbuilders

08 09 10 11 12   10 9 8 7 6 5 4 3 2 1

FOR A CATALOGUE OF ALL BOOKS PUBLISHED BY OSPREY MILITARY
AND AVIATION PLEASE CONTACT:

NORTH AMERICA
Osprey Direct, c/o Random House Distribution Center, 400 Hahn Road,
Westminster, MD 21157
Email: info@ospreydirect.com

ALL OTHER REGIONS
Osprey Direct UK, PO Box 140, Wellingborough,
Northants, NN8 2FA, UK
Email: info@ospreydirect.co.uk

www.ospreypublishing.com

ARTIST'S NOTE

Readers may care to note that the original paintings from which the
colour plates in this book were prepared are available for private sale.
All reproduction copyright whatsoever is retained by the Publishers.
All enquiries should be addressed to:

Peter Dennis, Fieldhead, The Park, Mansfield, Notts, NG18 2AT, UK

The Publishers regret that they can enter into no correspondence upon
this matter.

THE FORTRESS STUDY GROUP (FSG)

The object of the FSG is to advance the education of the public in the study
of all aspects of fortifications and their armaments, especially works
constructed to mount or resist artillery. The FSG holds an annual
conference in September over a long weekend with visits and evening
lectures, an annual tour abroad lasting about eight days, and an annual
Members' Day.

The FSG journal FORT is published annually, and its newsletter Casemate is
published three times a year. Membership is international. For further
details, please contact:

The Secretary, c/o 6 Lanark Place, London W9 1BS, UK

Website: www.fsgfort.com

THE WOODLAND TRUST

Osprey Publishing are supporting the Woodland Trust, the UK's leading
woodland conservation charity, by funding the dedication of trees.

CONTENTS

THE WALLS OF ROME

INTRODUCTION

The walls of Rome evolved over many centuries. The first early ditches and banks were thrown up by Rome's founding fathers. In the 4th century BC the Roman king Servius Tullius created what became known as the Servian wall, built of tufa stone and featuring a number of gates. Servius's creation would serve Rome well during the Second Punic War (218–201 BC), its formidable strength warding off siege by Hannibal's forces.

As the power of Rome grew, so did its capital, which expanded beyond the limits of the Servian wall. A long period of peace followed the founding of the empire, but in the third century AD new threats appeared. Barbarian raiders lay waiting on the borders of the empire, and economic crisis brought it almost to the point of collapse. The emperor Aurelian (AD 214–75), by stupendous military exertions, physically reunited the Roman empire under his iron rule. However, it was an empire battered and traumatized, and for the first time since Hannibal had ridden up to Porta Collina, the city of Rome itself had become vulnerable. This situation led to Aurelian's greatest monumental achievement – Aurelian's wall, built between AD 271 and 275. Still bearing his name to this day, it was erected to protect Rome following its narrow escape from a Germanic incursion that had penetrated deep into the Italian peninsula.

In AD 307, barely 30 years after the completion of the wall, the usurper Maxentius, faced with the prospect of defending Rome against two Roman armies – one led by Severus, the duly appointed western Caesar, and the other by Galerius, the eastern Augustus – reorganized the Aurelianic defences. This he did by doubling their height, blocking several lesser entrances and strengthening a number of the remaining gateways. According to Lactantius, he 'began the digging of a ditch but did not complete it' (*De mortibus persecutorum* 27).

A hundred or so years later, in the first decade of the 5th century AD, the defences were again reorganized by Stilicho, the regent of Honorius (r. AD 395–423). They proved an effective defence against two sieges by the Goths under Alaric, but failed to withstand the third attempt (AD 410). Nevertheless, Aurelian's wall continued to play a significant part in the history of Rome thereafter. Repaired twice in the mid 5th and early 6th centuries, the wall played a crucial role in the sieges and counter-sieges of the Gothic wars of Iustinianus (Justinian), during which it was twice repaired and strengthened by Belisarius (AD 537 and AD 546).

Although embellished, strengthened and restored many times over, it was Aurelian's original structure that remained the basis of Rome's defences down to the mid 19th century, when Garibaldi's pro-Italian unification forces (who had overthrown Pope Pius IX and declared Rome a republic) managed for some time to withstand the French army coming to the Pope's aid. Today the remains of his wall are still discernible along much of the original circuit. Aurelian's wall is arguably the best preserved of all city walls in the Roman empire, and even the present-day traveller cannot help but be impressed by the majesty of the imposing ruins.

Aurelian's wall along Viale Metronia between the Metrobia and Latina gates – a general view looking south. (Author's collection)

CHRONOLOGY

4th century BC	The 11km-long Servian wall is built around the city of Rome
AD 235	Murder of the emperor Severus Alexander – beginning of the period known as the 3rd Century Crisis
AD 244	First campaign of Shapur, King of Persia, against Rome
AD 248	The Roman emperor Philip the Arab celebrates the millennium of Rome
AD 249	Goths cross the Danube
AD 252	Shapur's second campaign against Rome – Antioch is sacked
AD 253	Goths invade the Balkans
AD 256	Third campaign of Shapur – destruction of Dura-Europus; Franks cross the lower Rhine
AD 260	Fourth campaign of Shapur against Rome; establishment of Gallic empire by breakaway provinces of Gaul, Britannia and Hispania
AD 267	The Heruli sack Athens
AD 269	The Alamanni invade Italy; Goths invade the Balkans, but Claudius defeats them at Naissus (Niš)

ROME'S EARLY DEFENCES

The Servian wall north-east of the Viminal in Piazza dei Cinquecento, a general view looking north-west. Observe the non-alignment of vertical join between two stretches of the wall. (Author's collection)

From its estuary, the River Tiber is navigable for a distance of a hundred kilometres or thereabouts. Far enough from the sea to protect its first inhabitants from the danger of piracy, the site of ancient Rome lay 20km upstream on the east bank of the river at its lowest crossing point. This convenient ford,

The walls of Rome, 312 BC

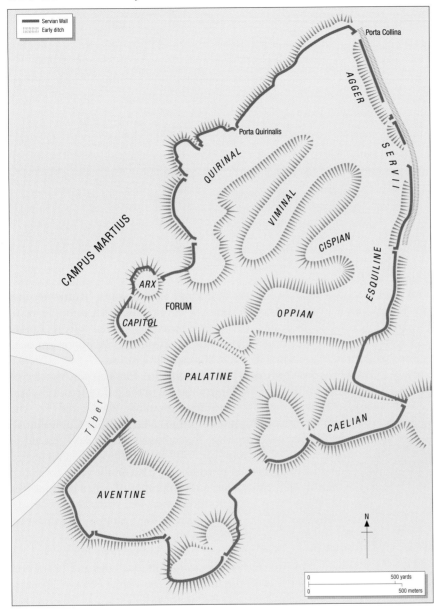

which lay south of an island in the river, was overlooked by a group of hills that harboured an adequate number of fresh-water springs. The hills themselves, which rise from the Latium Plain, were well wooded, fairly precipitous and defensible. The site, therefore, afforded some protection against floods, predators and the like.

Cicero may have once boasted 'that Romulus had from the outset the divine inspiration to make his city the seat of a mighty empire' (*De re publica* 2.10), but in the early days of its career nothing seemed to single out for future greatness a puny riverine settlement that long lay dormant. In these obscure times Rome was allied with other Latin settlements in Latium, and the seasonal battles that preoccupied the Latins were little more than internal squabbles over cattle rustling, water rights, and arable land.

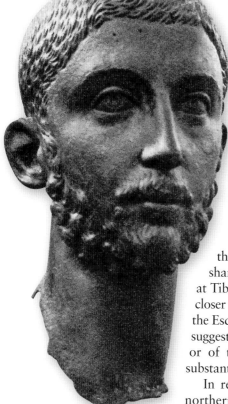

The seven hills

The poet Virgil, in reference to Romulus and Remus, says, 'Rome became the fairest thing in the world, embracing seven hills with a single wall' (*Georgics* 2.534–35). In reality, there were more than seven hills in Rome, and even the names of the traditional seven are disputed. The important ones for us, however, are listed in the following paragraphs.

A spur of the Quirinal, the **Capitoline** (or Capitol) was the site of the Capitoline temple, the largest temple in the Italo-Etruscan world and Rome's most important sanctuary. Dedicated to the Capitoline triad of Iuppiter Optimus Maximus (or Capitolinus), Iuno Regina and Minerva, this colossal temple was erected in the first year of the Republic (509 BC), and from then on served as the final destination of triumphs. Also on the same eminence were the Arx, or citadel, and a number of other temples like that dedicated to Mars, the god associated with the fury of war.

Another spur of the Quirinal, the spacious **Palatine** was the supposed site of Romulus's city. His hut, the *casa Romuli*, was kept there as a reserved place. Archaeology has proved the existence of Iron Age wattle-and-daub dwellings and burials on this hill at the time of the traditional founding of Rome (753 BC), and even earlier. Under the Republic the hill served as the residence of the aristocracy, while under the Principate it became the seat of imperial government, whence the origin of the word 'palace'.

As with the Palatine, evidence exists for Iron Age settlement on the **Esquiline** hill. Although the inhabitants of these hilltop villages shared a common Latial culture, finds from this site have their parallels at Tibur (Tivoli) and in southern Latium, those from the Palatine being closer to the 'Villanovan' warriors of the Alban hills in typology. Likewise, the Esquiline burials dated to circa 700 BC contain many weapons, which suggests an intrusion either of Fossa Grave culture people from Campania or of the Sabines, whom later Romans believed to have formed a substantial element in the early population.

In reality the **Quirinal** comprises two large flat-hills lying on the northern side of the ancient city. Although mainly residential, it also featured a number of sanctuaries, such as that dedicated to the mysterious Quirinus. The latter was identified by the Romans with both Mars and his miraculous son, the deified Romulus.

Known as the 'plebeian' hill, the **Aventine** sat outside the *pomoerium* – a ritual furrow made by a yoked bull and cow, so marking the area of a sacredly constituted city – until the early Principate. This hill was the site of the cult of Ceres, Libera and Liber Pater. The temple (496 BC), which was adorned with terracotta decorations executed by Greek artists, also functioned as the headquarters of the plebeian aediles and contained their archives as well as copies of *senatus consulta*, or decrees of the Senate.

First defences

Legend has it that Remus was killed when he mockingly leapt over the fortifications that Romulus was constructing on the Palatine. While Remus desired to build on the Aventine, Romulus much preferred the Palatine, and traces of a palisade defence dating to around that period have been found on this hill. As for the first defences of the city as a whole, it was said that they were erected during the phase of Etruscan domination.

The marble sarcophagus known as the 'Grande Ludovisi' (Rome, Palazzo Altemps, 8574), depicting Herennius Etruscus, son of Decius (r. AD 249–51), riding against the Goths at Abrittus. (Esther Carré)

Traditionally the last three kings of Rome were Etruscan, and it was the second of these, Servius Tullius (r. 579–534 BC), who was believed by later Romans to have constructed a massive stone wall around their city. The historian Livy (1.36.1, 44.3), writing under Augustus, reports that the project had been planned by Tarquinius Priscus but was eventually carried out by his son-in-law and successor. Livy, like other writers of the early Principate, believed that the wall of Servius Tullius could be identified with the stone enceinte that could still be seen in his day encircling the Capitol, Palatine, Caelian, Quirinal, Viminal, Aventine and part of the Esquiline. By the end of the 1st century BC this wall had long been out of use, appeared to be of great antiquity, and could thus be identified with the only early defences of the city mentioned in the historical tradition. But Livy and his fellow historians were mistaken.

The earliest bank-and-ditch defences of Rome, which may date to circa 540 BC, did not form a complete circuit around the city but only protected areas vulnerable to attack or raiding. The massive earth *agger* or rampart associated with the early ditch seems not to have been erected before about 480 BC, and probably no later than about 450 BC (Todd 1978: 14). It was during this period that Rome, along with other Latin cities, fought a series of petty and inconclusive wars with the neighbouring highlanders, the Aequi, the Volsci, and the Hernici, who threatened to overrun Latium. It was not until the end of the fifth century BC that the most formidable of these warlike mountain tribes, the Volsci, had been pushed out of the small, but rich coastal plain.

A marble bust (Paris, Musée du Louvre, MR511) of Gallienus (r. AD 253–68). The fact he survived the ignominious capture of his father and the widespread unrest that inevitably followed suggests that he was a singular man. (Esther Carré).

The Servian wall

In 390 BC, on the banks of the Allia (a tributary of the Tiber just 18km north of Rome), the Senones, under their war-chieftain Brennus, utterly trounced the Roman force sent to repel them, and Rome itself was subsequently sacked. But the revered Capitol hill stood firm and the so-called Servian wall actually belongs to the period immediately after the Gallic occupation, probably built between 378 and 350 BC.

Lying well within the circuit of Aurelian's later wall, stretches of this earlier wall still exist below and outside Roma Termini railway station. Interestingly enough, it is at the second of these two locations that the arrangement of blocks and the vertical join between two stretches of wall are not aligned – evidence of the workmanship of two building gangs. It was once thought that masons' marks on the blocks were of Greek origin, but they now seem to be archaic Latin and not Greek.

The Servian wall ran for some 11km and enclosed an area of roughly 426 hectares. The accompanying ditch was 29.6m wide and 9m deep. A flat berm of about 7m lay between ditch and wall. With a basal width of 3.6m, the wall itself stood about 10m high in places, and consisted of two quite distinct building stones cut into individual blocks. One was a grey tufa or *capellaccio*, so named because it covers like a hat layers of pozzolana in the subsoil, which was too light and breakable to be suitable for walling on its own. The other was a yellowish tufa of better quality, the so-called *Grotta Oscura*, which came from quarries near Veii (Isola Farnese), the Etruscan city that had been Rome's chief rival for supremacy in the Tiber valley until its annexation (396 BC).

The surviving blocks of tufa, grey or yellow, vary in length from 75cm to nearly 2.1m, in width from 45 to 66cm. On average they measure some 60cm in height. The courses were arranged alternately in headers and stretchers.

No projecting towers were provided either at the time of the original fortifications or later. The gateways seem to have been simple openings, the single entranceways being covered by towers placed against the internal wall face, a gate-type that persisted until the 1st century BC in the Italian peninsula (Todd 1978: 19).

There were later modifications to the Servian wall. According to Appian (*Bellum civilia* 1.66) the consuls of 87 BC, faced by the renegade army of Caius Marius, tried to strengthen the city defences by digging new ditches, restoring the wall and creating emplacements for artillery. The subsequent history of the wall, however, appears to have been one of progressive decay and dilapidation. Repairs to the Servian wall were not an option to Aurelian. It had largely been subsumed and obscured by subsequent building, and even by the reign of Augustus its exact line was uncertain.

THE AGE OF AURELIAN

The interval from the last Severan emperor (AD 235) to the Tetrarchy (AD 293) began and ended with strong government, but in between these lay a period of political instability and military stress. This half-century, which Rostovtzeff labelled the 'age of anarchy' and others have called the '3rd Century Crisis', saw at least 18 so-called legitimate emperors, and far more if the numerous usurpers who failed to establish themselves are counted. Nearly all met violent deaths, often at the hands of their own soldiers or in the course of another coup, after short reigns. Gallienus (r. AD 253–68) survived the longest, while Aurelian (r. AD 270–75), despite the brevity of his reign, was the most successful.

BELOW LEFT
A member of the re-enactment group Quinta equipped and dressed as a 3rd-century cavalryman. His bronze scale armour and wooden oval shield are based on evidence from Dura-Europus. (Author's collection)

BELOW RIGHT
The monumental arch carrying the Aqua Antoniniana, in a general view looking south in Via di San Sebastiano towards the rear of Porta Appia. Later Maxentian rebuilding would see this serving as an inner gate. (Author's collection)

The assassination (in March AD 235) and replacement of Severus Alexander by a tough career soldier from Thrace, Maximinus Thrax (r. AD 235–38), was a stark reminder that the empire needed emperors who knew the army. An equestrian outside the ruling clique, Maximinus had exploited the opportunities of the Severan army to gain numerous senior appointments.

However, the senatorial aristocracy could not agree to this particular appointment, and, after an eyeball-to-eyeball confrontation, they managed to face the army down. The subsequent run of emperors – the three Gordiani, Decius, Trebonianus Gallus, Valerianus and Gallienus – was one of 'gentlemen officers'. Yet their military misfortunes would finally destroy the prestige of the Augustan system, leaving military rule as the only alternative. Maximinus, the Thracian soldier of obscure birth and exclusively military experience, had set the trend whereby the army called the shots, putting forward their own commanders as new emperors.

As the 3rd century AD progressed, the number of senior army positions held by men of senatorial rank gradually declined, and this move away from the traditional mixed military and civilian career would gather momentum under Gallienus. Far more opportunities lay open to equestrians, especially those who campaigned under the emperor himself. The equestrian officers who now dominated the army were in many respects career soldiers, owing their advancement purely to their military record and the favour of the ruling emperor.

Perverse as it may seem, it was usually these men who plotted to murder an emperor and nominated a usurper from their group. Several of the most successful emperors of the second half of the century came from a virtual junta of professional officers from the Danubian provinces (hence the loose term 'Illyrian'), men of obscure origins but undoubted military ability who worked their way up through the crisis years to the highest commands and then doggedly fought invaders and each other.

The eastern front

During this period, a major change came about in Rome's eastern neighbour. The old Parthian kingdom of the Arsacids had been a quasi-feudal structure of powerful family domains and perpetual internal tensions, whose western regions were considerably influenced by Hellenic culture. The Parthians had been troublesome only if disturbed on their own ground.

Early in the third century the Arsacids were overthrown by a nationalist movement centred on the Iranian plateau, led by Ardashir of the house of Sassan and claiming spiritual descent from the ancient Achaemenid empire of Dareios and Xerxes. At home the Sassanids worked to build a strong, centralized Iranian state, purged of all foreign influences. Abroad the Sassanids made no secret of the fact that they intended to use this new-found sense of nationalism to re-create the former glories – and frontiers – of the Achaemenids. More formidable than the Parthians they had supplanted, the Sassanids constantly sought to alter the military status quo in Mesopotamia, Armenia and Syria.

Taking full advantage of the internal crisis within their empire, Shapur (r. AD 241–72), the son and successor to Ardashir, warred with great success against the Romans. The large-scale but ineffectual counter-offensive launched against Persia by Gordianus III (r. AD 238–44) ended in the emperor's death, perhaps at the hands of his Praetorian prefect Philip the Arab (r. AD 244–49), who succeeded him. The subsequent peace treaty between Shapur and the new emperor forced the Romans to pay tribute – half a million *denarii*, Shapur claims. A representation commemorating his humiliation of Rome survives in a rock-cut relief from Naqš-e Rustam. Two Roman emperors are shown submitting to the king on horseback, one of whom is Philip, who sues for peace on bended knee.

A further Persian offensive led to the occupation of Armenia, the devastation of Syria, and the capture of Antioch (AD 252), the great commercial capital of Hellenic Syria. Roman Antioch had never before fallen to an enemy. It was retaken with some difficulty, but henceforth Antioch was to be a piece in the strategic Rome–Persia game of chess, the theatre of which had now shifted alarmingly from the Euphrates, the boundary between the olive and the date, to only a short distance inland from the Mediterranean, the cradle of Graeco-Roman culture. The third campaign of Shapur culminated in the capture and destruction of the border fortress of Dura-Europus (AD 256). It was never reoccupied.

In the aforementioned rock-cut relief from Naqš-e Rustam the other emperor is Valerianus (r. AD 253–60), he and his army having surrendered to Shapur after being humiliated at Edessa (AD 260). Although Valerianus is portrayed standing up, his hands are held by the king, a reference to the fact he was taken prisoner, an ignominy that had never previously befallen a Roman emperor. To reinforce the insult, Shapur is said to have used the captive emperor as a human mounting block. One lurid story even claims that after Valerianus died in miserable servitude, he was flayed and his skin, dyed crimson, was stuffed with straw and put on public display.

With the Roman army of the east in utter disarray, it was left to Septimius Odaenathus, ruler of Palmyra, or Tadmor to give this Roman protectorate its Semitic name, to play the major role in forcing Shapur to withdraw from Roman territory. With his father disappeared into Persian captivity, Gallienus, who had been installed as co-emperor seven years earlier, now assumed full power. His area of effective control, however, was confined to Italy, Dalmatia, Greece, the western Danube and Africa, and though he managed to hold on to power for a further eight years, he was never able to reassert his authority over the whole empire.

The battle for the west
Independently but simultaneously, Rome's western neighbours were also changing. In response to both the aggression of newer peoples to the east and

---

A THE CASTRA PRAETORIA, C. AD 312

The Castra Praetoria, the camp for the Praetorian Guard, was erected in AD 23 and was a reflection of the rise to prominence of L. Aelius Seianus, commonly known as Sejanus, the highly ambitious Praetorian prefect under Tiberius. As Tacitus dryly notes, the 'command of the guard had hitherto been of slight importance. Sejanus enhanced it by concentrating the guard cohorts, scattered about Rome, in one camp' (*Annales* 4.2.1). The new camp stood at the north-eastern edge of the city on the Viminal hill and enclosed an area of just 16.72 hectares, about two-thirds the size of a contemporary legionary fortress accommodating two legions.

The original Tiberian curtains, of brick-faced concrete, stood some 3.5m high and supported a rampart-walk protected by battlements. These were then heightened, probably by Caracalla (r. AD 211–17), and subsequently repaired and given loftier towers by Gordianus III following the chaos of AD 238. The next major change was when Aurelian decided to fortify Rome, consequently incorporating the camp into his new city walls. This involved raising the height of the curtains almost to that of the towers of AD 238 and adding new battlements and wall-towers. These were again heightened as part of the Maxentian building programme.

When Constantinus took Rome after his victory at the Milvian Bridge, he emphasized the disbanding of the Praetorian Guard by demolishing the west wall of their camp, that which lies within the Aurelianic enceinte. The Praetorians, many of whom had perished along with their emperor as they retreated across the ill-fated pontoon bridge, had faithfully stood by Maxentius when Constantinus invaded Italy. The Praetorian Guard was never reformed.

In this scene we view the Castra Praetoria from the south-east, with Porta Chiusa, which has just been narrowed as part of the Maxentian modifications to the city walls, seen abutting the camp's southern defences.

A The Castra Praetoria, *c.* AD 312

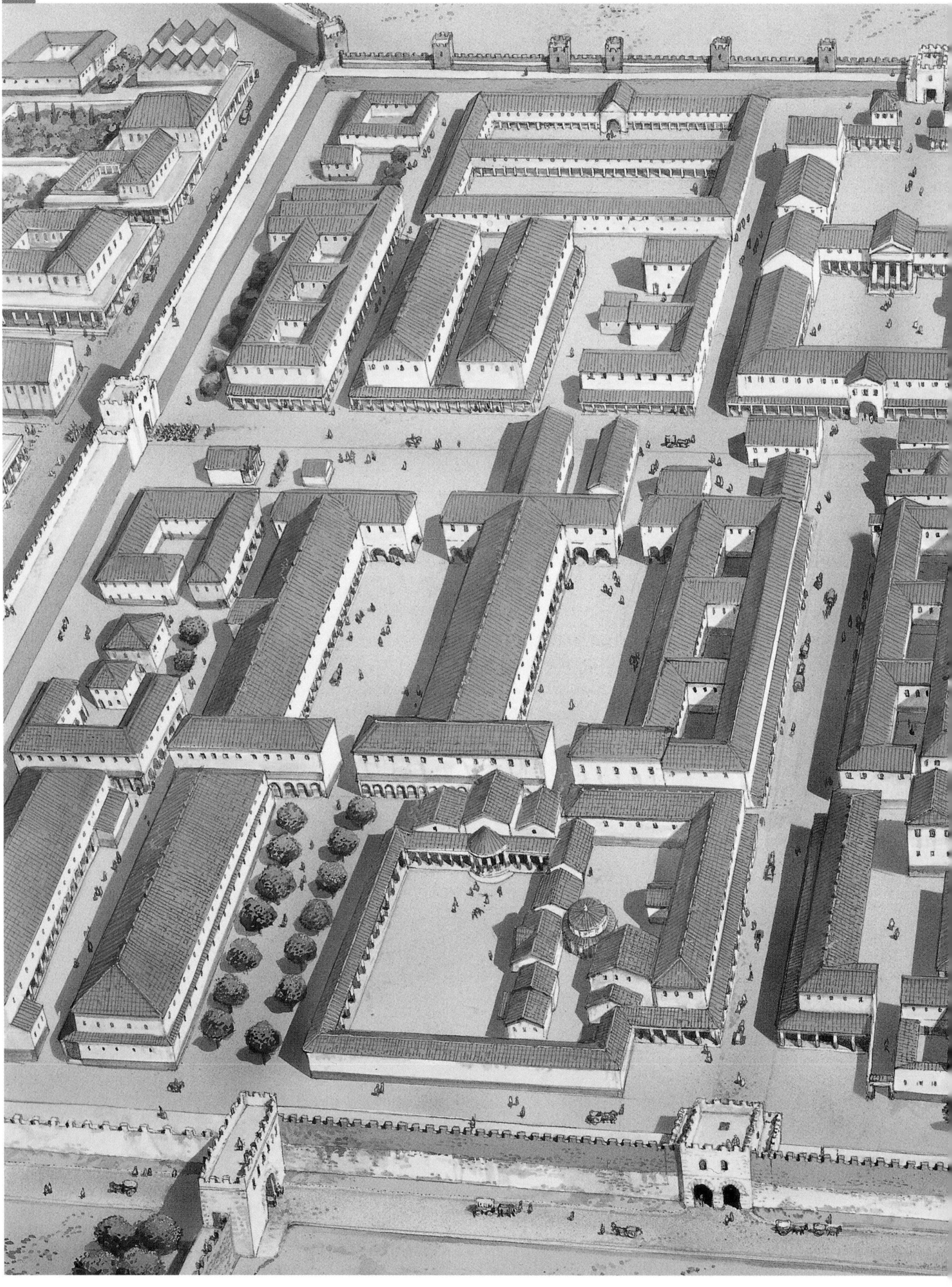

A Claudian monumental arch carrying the Aqua Claudia-Anio Novus, subsequently incorporated into Aurelian's wall to form the portals of Porta Praenestina-Labicana. (Author's collection)

the opportunities of what seemed limitless reserves of booty in the Roman provinces, the earlier Germanic tribes had fused into tribal confederations. By the early 3rd century three major groupings had emerged. The Suevic tribes of central Germania, with whom Caesar had first made contact (he had been unnerved by their ferocity), had formed into the Alamanni; those of the lower Rhine group into the Franks; and the sea-peoples at the mouth of the Elbe and Wesser into the Saxons. Though still of loose internal unity, the scale of military expedition these confederations could now mount was of an entirely new order, beyond what the existing Roman frontier defences had been designed to deal with.

Whether built in stone, timber, or earth and turf, whether consisting of a military way or a line of a river, these fixed frontier lines (*limites*) separated those outside from those within, those becoming romanized from their still barbarous neighbours. Trade and contact persisted, but it had been geographically channelled through supervised customs and crossing points. These physical barriers, therefore, had not been intended as impregnable fortifications or fighting platforms. On the contrary, they had been designed for surveillance and active, forward defence against anticipated raids or low-level incursions. As any fighting was intended to take place in the immediate zone beyond Roman territory, concentrated attacks could easily penetrate these defences.

The other area where the situation was changing to Rome's detriment was the lower Danube region. Starting in the late 2nd century the Gothic peoples in their tribal groupings had begun to shift slowly south-east from the Baltic littoral toward the Black Sea steppe. In AD 249, while Roman armies were occupied in civil war elsewhere, the Goths seized their opportunity and penetrated parts of Thrace and Asia Minor. Decius (r. AD 249–51), along with his son and heir, were both ambushed and cut down by this new foe. He was the first emperor to die in battle against enemies outside the empire.

Restoration and the defence of Rome

During the next two decades, although the empire was hard pressed and the imperial frontiers were broken by repeated and simultaneous hostile incursions, much was achieved in the name of Rome through the private enterprises of Postumus and his successors in the Gallic empire (AD 260–74), and in the east by the Palmyrene sub-empire of Odaenathus and Zenobia (AD 261–72). Yet it would seem as if the Roman world, split as it was into fragments, could not possibly survive. However, a series of formidable soldier-emperors were about to enter the fray.

First up in the sequence was Aurelian, who forcibly suppressed both separatist regimes but in doing so he was obliged to abandon Dacia north of the Danube to Gothic occupation. Perhaps the most telling sign that the winds of change had begun to blow was the emperor's momentous decision to provide Rome with city walls. His fellow Illyrian and successor Probus (r. AD 276–82), who extolled his memory and continued his policies, cleared Gaul, recently pacified but inadequately defended, of the Germanic invaders who took the opportunity to cross the upper Rhine in force when Aurelian was assassinated. In a double offensive Probus quickly turned the tide and expelled the invaders. He then carried the war across the Rhine in a punitive expedition deep into Germania. Though the resulting peace treaty allowed the Alamanni to retain the territory they had seized in the Rhine–Danube angle, it did attempt to disarm the tribes in the immediate frontier zone, as well as establishing a Roman military presence beyond the Rhine and securing large numbers of hostages and recruits. Probus also completed Aurelian's wall.

The man who built the wall

Like many of his recent predecessors, Lucius Domitius Aurelianus, to give him his full and proper name, was of humble provincial origins. He was born in Illyria of peasant stock (9 September AD 214 or 215), although his mother was said to have been a priestess of the sun-god, Sol Invictus (the 'Unconquered Sun'). This story was undoubtedly put out much later, when Sol Invictus became the most important deity for Aurelian, the divine protection to whom the emperor attributed the remarkable series of victories, especially in the east, which enabled him to restore the empire. Like a good many of his compatriots he joined the army, probably doing so around AD 235 – the same year Alexander Severus, the last of the Severan dynasty, was assassinated.

Aurelian appears to have been an exemplary soldier, who stood out from his fellow career soldiers even at a young age because of his martial qualities and single-minded determination. He subsequently rose through the ranks of the army. Two years before he became emperor he had already been a candidate for the post, but that time the honour went to another Illyrian soldier, Claudius II (r. AD 268–70). Aurelian had already achieved high military rank under Gallienus but helped organize the plot that destroyed him. In due course promoted to the position of overall commander of the cavalry, vacated by Claudius himself, he served with distinction against the Goths. By now his ruthless nature and relentless emphasis on military discipline had given rise to the nickname *manu ad ferrum*, 'hand-on-hilt' (*SHA* Aurelian 6.2). With the death of Claudius, in all probability the victim of a contagious disease, Aurelian was acclaimed emperor by the Danubian army (October AD 270).

Once invested with the purple he had to take immediate action: the situation on the northern frontier had become critical thanks to the simultaneous invasions of the Asding Vandals on the middle Danube and the Iuthungi into

The Papal fortress of Castel Sant'Angelo, which incorporates the cylindrical brick drum of the Mausoleum of Hadrian sited and built (AD 135–39) so as to impress passers-by on the Tiber. (Esther Carré)

'Super-heavy' cavalry

Palmyra had for long patrolled and policed the eastward caravan routes on which its prosperity depended. This was a pertinent preparation for military power. In other respects, also, the Semitic, semi-Hellenized Palmyra was well qualified to fill the role of Roman sword-bearer in the east. The Sassanid army relied extensively on noble cavalry, the *clibanarii* ('oven-men', cf. Greek *klibanos*, baking oven). These were horsemen, as their name suggests, fully encased in metal scale armour and mounted on horses protected by housings of leather or thick felt. The Palmyrene army also deployed heavy-armoured cavalry, the *cataphractarii*. By comparison, however, the Palmyrene *cataphractus* was a fully armoured man aboard a horse that was also usually armoured, but not necessarily so. Both Sassanid and Palmyrene horsemen, however, were armed with a heavy spear some 3.65m in length and held two-handed without a shield. The *contus* (Greek *kontós*) was a weapon for shock action, being driven home with the full thrust of the body behind it. The greater weight of men, horse and equipment meant their charge was considered to be more powerful than that of conventional cavalry.

northern Italy. The Iuthungi defeated Aurelian at Placentia (Piacenza) and advanced, apparently irresistibly, down the Via Aemilia into central Italy, threatening Rome itself. Panic gripped the city, for no significant force stood between it and the invaders.

Rome had long since outgrown and built over its ancient city walls. Besides, the vast empire and the strength of its legions had long been an ample buffer to protect the city, along with the rest of the Italian peninsula, from external threats. As the terrified, un-walled capital hurriedly made what preparations it could, the emperor regrouped his battered army and was able to turn back the invasion at Fanum Fortunae (Fano), then destroyed it completely in the open plains near Ticinum (Pavia). In recognition of this triumph he assumed the title Germanicus Maximus. Yet Aurelian was so alarmed that he ordered the immediate construction of a defensive circuit around Rome (spring AD 271), the famous wall that is still associated with his name to this day.[1]

During his short reign Aurelian had to deal with a number of challenges to his imperial authority, the greatest of which came in spring AD 272 when several eastern provinces of the empire were annexed by Septimia Zenobia, queen of Palmyra. By expanding into the power vacuum of the east, her late husband Odaenathus, though loyally defending the empire against Persia, had in fact adroitly created for himself a position of independence in the caravan city of Palmyra.

A later author, looking back in disdain on the recent past, may have moaned that 'the ruler of Palmyra thought himself our equal' (*Panegyrici Latini* 8.10), but in AD 261 Gallienus had belatedly appointed Odaenathus vice-regent of the east, declaring him *corrector totius orientis*; he could do little else. The Palmyrene prince thus held the supreme command of all the armed forces in the east, with full authority over the provincial governors of the entire region from Asia Minor to Egypt. As a result of this command Odaenathus assumed the title *dux Romanorum*.

[1] See especially, Zosimus 1.49.2, Aurelius Victor *Liber de Caesaribus* 35.7, *Epitome* 36.6, Eutropius 9.15.1, *SHA* Aurelian 39.2, Jerome *Chronicle* 223, and Malalas 12.30.

In AD 267 Odaenathus' talented widow Zenobia (Bath-Zabbai in Aramaic) inherited his position of unprecedented power in the Roman east and waited for an opportunity to break completely with Rome. And so while Claudius and Aurelius were preoccupied with the Goths in the mountains of northern Thrace, she easily secured Arabia and Iudaea (spring AD 270). Then as the Iuthungi overran northern Italy and threatened the capital, she overran much of Egypt (autumn AD 270). Next up was Syria and most of Asia Minor, including Galatia (spring AD 271).

Aurelian, though at first conciliatory, later felt obliged to reassert Roman authority. After assembling a substantial expeditionary force in Asia Minor, he quickly vanquished the formidable cavalry-army of Zenobia in two battles. Zabdas (Zabda), Zenobia's general, was unable to hold Antioch (spring AD 272) and made a second stand at Emesa (Homs). Here the Palmyrene *cataphractarii* drove Aurelian's cavalry from the field, but the emperor won the battle during their absence and the remnants of the Palmyrene forces soon found themselves beleaguered in Palmyra.

Palmyra fell to Aurelian, despite Zenobia's efforts to involve Persia (summer AD 272). Zenobia was captured as she attempted to cross the Euphrates, but Aurelian spared her along with the city. The following year, after successfully defeating the Carpi along the Danube, the emperor was incensed when he heard that Palmyra had revolted and had slaughtered the Roman garrison installed

A close-up shot of Via Ardeatina, running south-east out of Porta Ardeatina, showing the *agger* or embankment, basalt metalling, and one of the gutters. (Author's collection)

there. He then executed a well-conducted foray that surprised the defenders, captured Palmyra, and mercilessly razed it. From that time the City of Palms sank into quiet oblivion to become an unimportant provincial town on the outskirts of the Roman empire. Zenobia, however, lived to walk in Aurelian's triumph (autumn AD 274) and ended her life as a fashionable Roman hostess with a pension and a villa.

With the affairs of the east firmly under his grip, Aurelian now turned his attention west (summer AD 274), specifically to the sub-empire of Gaul, Britannia and Iberia, which had been pursuing its independent course with some success for well over a decade. The emperor Postumus (r. AD 260–68) had been lynched by his own soldiers and the present ruler, Tetricus, believed that he could rule over his own Gallic empire just as Postumus had done before. Together with his young son of the same name he had managed to hold out for nearly three years, but now it was all up for him, though Aurelian did spare the lives of father and son – they both featured alongside Zenobia as the star attraction in Aurelian's magnificent extravaganza (Eutropius 9.13.2) – even going so far as re-confirming their senatorial status and granting the elder Tetricus a civil administrative post in Italy.

The political aberration of parallel rulers holding sway in different parts of the empire, which had persisted for nearly a decade and a half since the capture of Valerianus, was at an end. By the springtime of AD 275 unity seemed to have been restored to the empire. Aurelian had rightly taken the title *restitutor orbis*, 'restorer of the world', and everything seemed to suggest that the burly soldier-emperor was in complete control of things. He was even able to work on bolstering the economy through the most comprehensive overhaul of the imperial monetary system since the reign of Augustus. But for an emperor of the 3rd century, danger was always lurking just around the corner. Aurelian, who was marching eastward through Thrace to wage war on the Persians, was assassinated in the vicinity of Byzantium by his senior officers: so disappeared from history an emperor who had done everything to halt the decline of the empire.

Aurelian reigned for just five years and two months, but under his energetic rule the empire had been granted time to recover. Like Gallienus before him, Aurelian realized that the empire could only be protected if the static concepts of frontier defence were abandoned. With the deployment of field armies – Aurelian placed his confidence in the cavalry corps developed by Gallienus – there was now a conscious shift towards strategic mobility.

Aurelian's army

Internal instability had led to losses and defeats on all imperial frontiers and further encouraged local rebellions and military coups. Each emperor was required to campaign with little respite, since he could rarely afford to entrust the command of an army to a potential rival. When the emperor was required to campaign in one theatre of operations there was a great danger that other parts of the empire, feeling their own difficulties were being neglected, would create a rival. It was Gallienus who developed the weapon with which his Illyrian successors fought off Persians and Germanic tribes alike. This was what was known at the time as the 'elite army', namely a mobile force not committed to frontier defence. Made up of detachments (*vexillationes*) drawn from frontier units in Britannia and on the Rhine and Danube, this force operated independently and was perhaps the forerunner of the 4th-century *comitatenses*, or field armies.

The elite army

In the 50 years from the assassination of Alexander Severus to the temporary establishment of peace under Diocletianus, there was an 'elite army' permanently in the field. It was not always exactly the same army that consisted of exactly the same units. Successive emperors commanded armies composed of *vexillationes* from various different *legiones*, *cohortes* and *alae* of the provincial garrisons, the choice of troops depending of course upon the location of the almost perpetual wars and availability of manpower. Although nothing new, these *vexillationes*, as opposed to whole legions, had now become the standard combat formation.

The legion-based army of the Principate was designed primarily for delivering powerful offensive strikes at specific fixed targets. In the military context of the 3rd century, however, cavalry were fast becoming increasingly important in the defence of the empire and the struggle against rebels and usurpers. In both cases, mobility was essential.

To move an army from the Rhine to Rome took eight weeks – and to the Euphrates six months. Roman armies could no longer choose the time and place for their battles and mount a campaign with the advantage of time and planning on their side. The days of overt imperialism were over, a time when tribal aggression in any particular sector could be anticipated and neutralized outside Roman territory. Now the encounters were all too often sprung upon the emperor, by barbarians or by fellow Romans – sometimes simultaneously.

Gallienus's cavalry corps

Sometime around AD 255, when he was defending the Rhine frontier and there was a desperate need for rapid movement, Gallienus created a cavalry corps (de Blois 1976: 26). He almost certainly employed the corps as part of the army hastily gathered together for the campaign against the Alamanni some three years later. This 'elite army' was quite small, Gallienus having assembled *vexillationes* from the static garrisons on the Rhine, Britannia, Pannonia and Noricum, and brought *legio II Parthica* and the Praetorian Guard from Rome. From about AD 260 the cavalry corps was stationed at Mediolanum (Milan) under its single commander Aureolus, whose task, according to Zosimus (1.40.1), was to prevent the anticipated invasion by Postumus across the Alps from Gaul. The threat from the breakaway Gallic empire was probably not Gallienus's sole concern, however. The much more pressing reason for occupying Mediolanum in considerable strength, with emphasis on mobility, was the threat posed by the Alamanni immediately to the north in Raetia.

Though little is known about Gallienus's cavalry corps, it is likely that he seconded his troopers, undoubtedly horsemen of proven ability and skill, from existing units. It is known, for instance, that he extracted men from the mounted troops stationed in Dalmatia, the *equites Dalmatae*. Besides the regular *alae* and *cohortes equitatae* of the provincial garrisons, there were tribal contingents available also, such as the Mauri and Osrhoeni recruited by Alexander Severus in the east and brought to Rhine by Maximinus (*SHA Severus Alexander* 61.8, two *Maximini* 11.1, 7, Herodian 7.2.1–2). If they had enlisted for 25 years, they would have had a few years left to serve when Gallienus was seeking experienced horsemen (Southern–Dixon 2000: 12).

These horsemen were certainly brigaded together, but it is not known how they fought together on the battlefield. They seem to have employed different, specialized fighting techniques: the Mauri, nimble horsemen of legendary ferocity, were armed with javelins and the Osrhoeni, as befitting eastern horse-archers, with the powerful composite bow. Individual units may have been employed for different purposes, but the cavalry had only one commander, and this unity of command implies unity of operation. It also facilitated potential usurpations, since the commander of the cavalry corps had an excellent power base at his immediate disposal. As the most influential, hence most dangerous, subject in the embattled empire, the brilliant but capricious Aureolus could not resist the temptation to rebel against Gallienus, but he did not succeed to the throne; he merely cleared the path to it for Claudius, before being murdered himself.

The questions of whether the cavalry corps survived and whether Gallienus is really the innovator behind the 4th-century *comitatenses* are unanswerable, given the lack of contemporaneous evidence. A Byzantine chronicler, George Cedrenus, states quite firmly that the emperor was the founder of the first cavalry army, emphasizing 'the Roman army having previously been largely infantry' (*Compendium Historiarum* 454). Not all scholars would agree with his judgement, Tomlin (1989: 223), for instance, pointing out the independent cavalry forces that won victories for Trajan and Septimius Severus. The Byzantine writers had the benefit of hindsight and were accustomed to the use of cavalry armies from the time of Constantinus (r. AD 306–37) onwards; therefore it seems natural that any army composed purely of horsemen, which was moreover not part of any provincial garrison but answerable via its commander to the emperor alone, would seem to be a direct forerunner of the later cavalry armies.

De Blois (1976: 28) points out that the cavalry were no longer stationed at Mediolanum after about AD 285. By this time the Gallic empire had been quashed and Gaul was back again in the fold of the empire. De Blois takes the view that Gallienus's cavalry corps was not unlike the *vexillationes* employed in other wars, brought together temporarily for a specific purpose and disbanded when that purpose had been fulfilled. This view is shared by Ferrill (1986: 32), who thinks that Gallienus had no permanent policy in mind.

Southern and Dixon (2000: 13), on the other hand, raise a minor point that possibly contradicts this thesis and, in part, goes some way to rehabilitate the opinions of older scholars. Numismatic evidence demonstrates that the title given to Gallienus's cavalry corps was simply *equites*, rather than *ala* or the less permanent *vexillatio*. This use of the non-specific title possibly signifies that the corps was not intended to function after the fashion of the provincial *alae*, but at the same time it was not intended to function as another *vexillatio*. An inscription (*ILS* 569), dating to the year after Gallienus' murder, preserves this distinction, whatever it may mean, by listing *vexillationes adque equites* side by side. Yet, given the current state of evidence, it is not possible to refute or endorse the theory that Gallienus's cavalry corps was intended to form the first permanent cavalry army, the precursor of the *comitatenses*.

Gallienus originally developed the cavalry corps not from any comprehensive plan but in answer to his need for mobility on the Rhine, and then adapted the use of this mobile force to the multiple desperate situations facing him in the ensuing years. Legend claimed there had been 30 usurpers during his comparatively long reign, so the permanent survival of the cavalry corps could have been almost accidental at first, then regularized by custom afterwards. Southern and Dixon (2000: 14) suggest that its disappearance from Mediolanum is a possible indication that after AD 285 the corps was permanently in the field with the ruling emperor, employed in a similar fashion to the later *comitatenses*.

It may have been used by Claudius against the Alamanni, who invaded Italy through Raetia just after Gallienus's death. After initial defeats, Claudius appointed Aurelian 'commander-in-chief of the cavalry' (*SHA* Aurelian 18.1). There is no

Aurelian's wall along Viale di Porta Ardeatina between the Ardeatina and Appia gates, in a general view looking north that shows the regularly placed, projecting towers. (Author's collection)

The brick-faced concrete construction on the interior of a tower in Viale Giotte. Once properly set, it created a homogeneous mass that was less vulnerable to collapse than dry stone construction. (Author's collection)

proof that this command embraced Gallienus's cavalry corps, but it is at least likely that the remnants of it formed the rump of Aurelian's cavalry corps. There were certainly Dalmatian and Mauritanian cavalry units in his corps, just as there were in that of Gallienus. When Claudius despatched Aurelius to tackle the Gothic incursion of AD 269, his sizeable command certainly included the Dalmatian cavalry, which he used to great effect (Zosimus 1.45, *SHA* Claudius 11.3-9). Likewise Aurelian, as emperor, used not only the Dalmatians that had distinguished themselves under his leadership in the Gothic wars, but also Mauritanian horsemen to defeat the formidable Palmyrene *cataphractarii* (Zosimus 1.50.3-51.1).

A close-up shot of the west gate-tower of Porta Appia, showing the rampart-walk and battlements; note the height of the merlons. (Author's collection)

AURELIAN'S WALL

Aurelian's Rome

The 3rd century was above all a world dominated by armies. The emperors, created by these armies, were almost exclusively men of comparatively humble origin promoted on merit rather than social standing. In this martial climate, the senatorial aristocracy in Rome lost its pride of place. It no longer retained the sole access to political power, still less to control it. But now emperors no longer resided or were made at Rome. It was more practical for emperors raised in the field surrounded by their own troops, as most were, to appoint men from among their own kind, men like Aurelian himself. Following the general rule of the day, his accession had been an army coup, set in a military camp, and marked by ceremonial acclamations hailing the new emperor as *imperator*.

From the late 2nd century onwards the centre of power in the empire had become increasingly peripatetic, following the emperor as he spent even more time in the frontier zones. 'Rome', as the conceptual capital of the empire, thus became divorced from the physical city of seven hills, or, as Herodian properly puts it, 'Rome is where the emperor is' (1.6.5, cf. 2.10.9). The emperor's presence on campaign often necessitated the elevation of his provincial headquarters into *de facto* regional 'capitals', that is, imperial centres in the frontier zones, often associated with regional branches of the imperial mint. This process would ultimately culminate in the foundation of Constantinople as a 'New Rome' on the Bosporus.

All roads did not lead to the old Rome, yet the attention that Aurelian lavished on major building projects in Rome, which not only included the city walls but also a new camp to house the urban cohorts, is not so much a comment on the strategic or political importance of the capital as on his conviction that Rome still mattered symbolically. Before he departed for the Danubian front to deal with a renewed barbarian threat, the emperor personally oversaw the necessary arrangements for the building project to get swiftly under way (*SHA* Aurelian 22.1, Malalas 12.30).

Tracing the circuit

To have surrounded the whole of 3rd-century Rome with an enceinte would have made neither economic nor strategic sense. Even so, the circuit of the new city walls was nearly 19km in length, and the huge expanse (2,500 hectares) now enclosed more than double the area surrounded by the Servian wall, most of the 14 Augustan regions of the city and all the major structures of importance. At no point did the new wall follow the line of the old, though it does, however, follow an earlier boundary. On the north and south sides at least, the wall respects quite closely the old customs or toll boundary of the city, which dates back to the reign of Vespasianus and had been marked out by boundary stones in the late Antonine period (*CIL* 6.1016a-c, 31227).

Naturally, the course of the wall was dictated by the needs of defensive strategy. A salient on the south incorporated a stretch of the Via Appia within the wall so as to protect the Aqua Antoniniana and fortify the northern lip of the Almo valley, which would have otherwise dominated the city defences. To the west across the Tiber, part of the XIV region on the west bank, an area roughly corresponding to modern Trastevere, was enclosed in a massive salient that stretched to the top of the Janiculum. It was on the slopes of this hill that the city's flour mills were located. They were powered by trans-Tibertine aqueducts coming over the brow of the hill, the Aqua Traiana and the Aqua Alsietina. Needless to say, as Procopius (*Wars* 5.19.8–9) points out, the mills and their associated water supplies were of profound logistical significance with regards to the bread supply of the city, the location of which helped to dictate the line of Aurelian's wall in this sector.

Only in the east did the line of the wall certainly abandon the customs boundary altogether, enclosing a considerable additional area bounded in the north-east by the Castra Praetoria, or Praetorian Camp, and in the south-east by an important system of aqueducts. The aquae Claudia-Anio Novus and Marcia-Tepula-Iulia provided a substantial part of the city's water supply and in themselves they would have offered a tactical vantage point to an enemy had not the wall been set to pass along their outer side. Except for a short stretch either side of Porta Praenestina-Labicana, the aqueducts were not physically incorporated within the structure of the wall as such, and thus economy of resources cannot be cited as the reason for the choice of line. Wherever deviations from the old customs boundary can be postulated, therefore, there existed sound strategic reasons for the line chosen (Watson 2004: 146).

Strategy also demanded that the river bank itself should be strengthened to connect the fortifications on each side of the Tiber. Two stretches of Aurelian's wall were therefore built on the topmost of three embankment tiers along the east bank: one in the south, of some 800m; the other approximately three times as long, linking the trans-Tibertine walls with Porta Flaminia in the north. The circuit thus incorporated all the urban bridges within the fortifications, with the possible exception of the Pons Aelius and perhaps the Pons Neronianus, if the latter had not already been demolished by Aurelian's time.

Though the evidence is wanting, it is highly likely that the fortifications reached across the Pons Aelius, incorporating the great cylindrical drum of the Mausoleum of Hadrian (now Castel Sant'Angelo) on the west bank, thereby making a bridgehead of this imposing structure. This is certainly the case in Procopius's day, when this structure was a bridgehead fort surrounded by strong walls, and as such attracted the attention of the besieging Ostrogoths. When it was first turned over to its new function Procopius does not say, but as the dramatic events he describes first-hand make plain (*Wars* 5.22.12–25), it would have made little strategic sense for Aurelian to have left the mausoleum and the bridge outside the fortification system.

Design of the wall
During the late 3rd century, Roman defensive architecture as a whole was to change. The empire, once the aggressor, found itself increasingly on the defensive. New defences, both military and urban, were built on an altogether massive scale. Curtains became thicker and higher than had previously been the norm, and increases in scale were accompanied by architectural innovations. Solid, forward-projecting towers, usually sited less than 30m apart, studded the new fortification circuits, thus providing stable firing platforms for light

An interior view of Aurelian's wall in Viale Carlo Felice between the Amphitheatrum Castrense and Porta Asinaria, showing the Maxentian galleried wall sitting upon the Aurelianic gallery. (Author's collection)

25

artillery. Gateways, of course, were potential weak points. They, too, became more heavily defended, often with flanking towers or towers on either side of a single, narrow entranceway. Usually a broad ditch, or ditches, surrounded the whole work.

One very important factor for this change in defensive architecture was the shift in the nature and location of warfare. Whereas warfare had previously been conducted on or beyond the frontiers of the empire, in the 3rd century, as we have already discussed, the theatre of war shifted to being largely within the provinces. For instance, the cities in Gaul, when rebuilding and castramentation took place after the barbarian invasions of the middle decades of the century, saw their urban space typically contract. This reduction in size is illustrated by Augustodunum (Autun), whose Augustan walls enclosing 200 hectares were now supplemented by an inner circuit covering just ten. The larger circuit continued to stand, but it had probably little defensive value. While in the Principate cities had not required circuits, they now started to acquire powerful, as opposed to merely prestigious, urban fortifications and to change their appearance into the walled city typical of late antiquity.

The method of construction

The main structure of Aurelian's wall was built using a functional and simple wall construction method. Free-standing, it was built of a compact core of irregularly shaped pieces of tufa and travertine held in a cement (*caementa*) of lime and pozzolana, which on setting became iron-hard. Unusually for this date, both the aggregate of the core and even that for the foundation consisted of new material and not rubble taken from demolished buildings, monumental sculptures and tombstones. Concrete, or *opus caementicium* as it was then called, had been in use since the end of the 3rd century BC, and for Aurelian's wall it was faced, inside and out, with bricks or tiles set in mortar.

Known as *opus latericia*, this type of wall facing had evolved in the 1st century BC with the use of broken tiles and sun-dried bricks (*lateres*). The unfired bricks were substituted in the Augustan period bykiln-baked bricks (*testae*). These bricks were mass produced on an industrial scale, manufactured in square shapes of

An exterior view of Porta Appia, looking north in Via Appia Antica. Originally, like all Type I gateways, Porta Appia was equipped with a double-span archway flanked by round-fronted towers. (Author's collection)

various sizes and then sub-divided, usually into smaller triangles, and placed in position with the vertex at the inner concrete core of a wall and the base facing outwards. For Aurelian's wall the bricks and tiles, as Vitruvius (2.3.2) recommends, were reused and thus weathered. Most were Hadrianic, as indicated by the stamps, though some were as late as Severan, and probably came from buildings demolished to make room for the passage of the wall.

There was a potential weakness in this type of wall construction method, specifically at the junction of the shallow facing and the concrete core. Although the builders of Aurelian's wall used material for their facing with a long tail that could be well held by the core, as an extra security, one or several horizontal bonding courses were also used at regular vertical intervals. The material used in these courses was large tiles. These reached further back into the core than the facing bricks or tiles themselves, and helped to key in the facing more securely. Bonding courses, a minor but nonetheless significant change in defensive architecture, also served as a means of levelling a wall during its construction. The wall itself was constructed in short segments, measuring

An exterior view of Porta Ostiensis East, looking north-north-west in Piazzale Ostiense. Like Porta Appia, this was a Type I gateway and thus served a main axial road into Rome. (Author's collection)

4.5 to 6m in length, 1.3 to 1.8m in height and extending right through the thickness (Richmond 1930: 60). The absence of putlog holes implies the builders worked from the wall top as construction proceeded, or perhaps from free-standing scaffolding.

All things being equal, the resulting structure was tough and durable, capable of withstanding the ravages of weather and the shock of earthquake. Yet the quality of workmanship varied considerably. It is interesting to note that Vitruvius (2.8.7), a military engineer under Caesar and later Octavian (the future Augustus), complains that in his day builders, eager for speedy results, attended only to the facing and botched the core. Such a common human weakness was still apparent in Aurelian's day. In places, great care was taken to pack in the concrete tightly behind the facing. For much of the circuit, however, the haste of the construction and the inexperience of the builders are evident. In places, for instance, the bricks and tiles were of insufficient depth to permit proper bonding to the core, allowing the facing to sheer off over time.

Human resources

As in times of the Principate, the most obvious labour force for this type of project would have been the army. Aurelian, however, could not spare the manpower. According to the Byzantine writer John Malalas (12.30), active in the late 6th century, Aurelian therefore drafted the city guilds (*collegia*) to carry out the actual building work, perhaps under the supervision of a small cadre of military personnel. The use of the *collegia* as conscript labour was an innovation imposed on Aurelian by the circumstances of the time, but in the next century it would become increasingly common. In return for this undertaking, the *collegia* were granted the right to bear the name *Aureliani* in their official titles.

The simplicity of the overall design and the high level of standardization imposed on almost every aspect of construction were necessary to workmen who lacked the expertise and discipline of military engineering. Not surprisingly this simplicity and uniformity also helped to save time and expense, even if, like Rome, the wall was not built in a day.

Certainly, the project as a whole occupied the rest of Aurelian's reign, and indeed remained unfinished at his death in the autumn of AD 275. Malalas (12.30) states that Aurelian's wall was finished in a very short time, and implies that this happened within the emperor's reign, but Zosimus says (1.49.2) it was finally completed under Probus, who, after all, was a man very much in Aurelian's own mould. Probably the bulk of the project was completed under Aurelian but the whole not actually finished until the reign of Probus, a period of six years from conception to completion.

Exterior view of Porta Latina, looking west in Via Latina. This Type II gateway was altered under Honorius, whereby the single-span archway was reduced in width. The right-hand tower is original, but that on the left is Belisarian in date. (Author's collection)

The anatomy of the wall

In terms of defensive architecture Aurelian's wall was a product of its time, with both new and old elements mingled together. As we shall see, the rectangular towers and simple gateways owe nothing to the fresh ideas of fortification design at this very date taking shape in the western provinces. However, as noted already, the relative simplicity of the Aurelianic defences was due to their construction by the city *collegia*, civilians working in the only tradition known to them. Had they been built by military engineers, many more of the new modes of fortification would be manifest in the walls of Rome. Nevertheless, the circuit is one of the earliest in which close positioning of wall-towers and the arrangement of their upper works clearly demonstrates the role envisaged for defensive artillery.

Curtains

The foundations were laid in a 4m-wide trench, and of varying depth, revetted by wooden shuttering, which was in many sections left *in situ* as the concrete hardened. To accommodate undulating terrain, the footings were sometimes stepped, faced with tiles or blocks of tufa and left exposed above ground. In this way the top of the foundation was maintained at a fairly uniform level.

OPPOSITE PAGE
Interior view of Porta Tiburtina, looking south-east in Piazza di San Lorenzo. This Type II gateway began life as a monumental arch, seen here, erected under Augustus (r. 27 BC–AD 14) to carry the Aqua Iulia-Tepula-Marcia over Via Tiburtina. (Author's collection)

Incorporating the monumental arches carrying the Aqua Claudia-Anio Novus over viae Praenestina and Labicana, Porta Praenestina-Labicana was effectively a double-Type II gateway. This interior view shows the architrave inscription celebrating its imperial sponsor, Claudius I. (Author's collection)

Above this solid base the curtain-wall of brick- or tile-faced concrete stood 6.1m high and 3.65m thick, which in turn supported a rampart-walk made of fine concrete with a string-course of tiles on the outer face of the wall. The rampart-walk was protected by wide-set and somewhat irregular battlements, which raised the total height of the superstructure from the outside to just short of 8m (Watson 2004: 147).

On certain sections of the circuit the structure of the curtains are of a quite different type. Either side of Porta Asinaria in the south, and east of Porta Pinciana in the north, the curtain-wall is solid only to a height of about 3m, upon which base was constructed a low, barrel-vaulted gallery supporting the rampart-walk and the battlements at the standard height. The gallery was equipped with loopholes for archers. It is not clear why this is so, and the difference may represent nothing more than the work of different labourers, perhaps even military personnel. Still, as we shall see, this was a striking anticipation, albeit on a much smaller scale, of the later Maxentian curtains.

For economic and strategic reasons many pre-existing buildings and older structures were incorporated within the fabric of Aurelian's wall. Of these, the most outstanding are: the retaining walls of the Horti Aciliorum and Horti Sallustiani in the north; the curtains and towers of the Castra Praetoria, which had to be raised (the camp itself still retained its military function); the side of a tenement block near the north-east angle of the Castra Praetoria, embedded in the wall fabric with its windows filled in; a short stretch of the Aqua Claudia-Anio Novus on either side of Porta Praenestina-Labicana; the early 3rd-century Amphitheatrum Castrense, which still functioned but had its southern arcades bricked up; and several tombs, most notably that of M. Virgilius Eurysaces and the Pyramid of Caius Cestius. As already noted, the Mausoleum of Hadrian may also be counted in this list. In total, approximately one-tenth of the entire circuit was accounted for in this way (Todd 1978: 28).

Of those parts that were truly Aurelianic, the most distinctive deviation from the blue print was to be seen in the riverine curtains. Confident that the river afforded sufficient security, the circuit had been erected here almost entirely devoid of towers, at any rate for long stretches. Yet according to the experienced military judgement of Procopius (in all probability this was actually the opinion of his beloved commander Belisarius), the riverside sector 'was especially vulnerable' (*Wars* 6.9.16).

Towers

For the greater part of its length, the circuit was studded at regular intervals of about every 30m by a system of 381 towers. With very few exceptions the Aurelianic towers were simple, in keeping with the economic policy adopted by the planners. They were uniformly rectangular in shape, measuring 7.6m across, projecting 3.35m in front of the curtains and flushed with the back, and rising some 4.5m above the rampart-walk. In most cases the towers consisted of a solid mass of brick- or tile-faced concrete to the level of the rampart-walk, from where there was access to a triple barrel-vaulted chamber with a central stairway leading up to a crenellated open terrace (Watson 2004: 147).

The chambers were usually equipped with two round-headed windows facing forward for the use of *ballistae*, with another such window on either side to allow these machines to swivel 90 degrees. It is important to note that the standard *ballista* of this period was a twin-armed torsion engine, which shot bolts (*iaculi*) and not stones (Marsden 1969: 188–89). These projectiles normally had an iron head, pyramidal in cross-section, which was fixed to a wooden body, mainly ash, equipped with three maple wood vanes or flights.

On the galleried sections of the wall, the towers were differently planned, though their external aspect remained largely unaltered. These towers also projected 3.5m in front of the curtain-wall, but were only solid up to the height of the gallery floor, that is, to about 3m. From the gallery, which passed through the rear of the tower, a staircase ran round the other three sides and gave access to an upper-level artillery chamber and the rampart-walk. The chamber was of the same dimensions as the majority of other towers, but its internal arrangement was cramped by the staircase (Todd 1978: 32–33).

In neither type of tower was there any means of access from the ground to the upper chamber or the rampart-walk. Access to the upper works could only be gained by stairs associated with gateways. With access to the wall solely confined to gate-towers, the defenders could pass along it only by the rampart-walk. The principal aim in this was to control the unwanted interference of civilians, whose presence might impede the defenders during an emergency.

Gateways

Aurelian's wall originally had 18 gateways, of which nine have survived, though it was actually pierced by as many as 29 entrances if the numerous posterns (small side gates) are taken into account. As the builders were clearly working to a carefully predetermined plan, these openings may be divided into four distinct types.

First there were four great gateways (Type I: the Flaminia, Appia, Ostiensis East and Portuensis gates), each originally equipped with a double-span archway set in a two-storied curtain-wall faced with travertine and flanked by round-fronted towers. These gateways served the four main axial roads leading into the city: the Via Flaminia in from the north, the Via Appia from the south and the two main roads either side of the Tiber that led to the two ports of Rome, the Via Ostiensis on the east bank and the Via Portuensis on the west bank.

LEFT
An exterior view of Porta Ardeatina, looking north-west in Via Ardeatina. Like all Type III gateways, Porta Ardeatina was simply a glorified postern. (Author's collection)

RIGHT
An exterior view of the blocked postern opposite Via dei Marsi, looking south-west in Via di Porta Labicana. Observe the double relieving arches above the travertine door-head. (Author's collection)

The second category (Type II: the Salaria, Nomentana, Tiburtina and Latina gates) consisted of a single-span archway, again set in a two-storied curtain-wall, but without the travertine facing, and flanked by round-fronted towers. These gateways served roads of secondary importance, the viae Salaria, Nomentana, Tiburtina and Latina. Of interest is Porta Tiburtina on the east of the city. This started life as a monumental arch of the Augustan period erected to carry the Aqua Iulia-Tepula-Marcia over Via Tiburtina, which was then incorporated into Aurelian's wall.

Porta Praenestina-Labicana, which incorporated and transformed the monumental arches that Claudius I had erected to carry the Aqua Claudia-Anio Novus over the viae Praenestina and Labicana, was a special case. The two roads made for separate arches in the aqueduct, the funerary monument of M. Virgilius Eurysaces, *pistor et redemptor* ('baker and public contractor'), lying between them. It was, therefore, effectively two gateways of Type II juxtaposed

B CURTAIN WALL CROSS SECTIONS

1. The Aurelianic solid curtain-wall. Curtains formed the core of the new defences of Rome. These consisted of brick- or tile-faced concrete standing 6.1m high and 3.65m thick. This supported a rampart-walk made of fine concrete, with a string-course of tiles on the outer face of the wall. The rampart-walk was protected by wide-set and somewhat irregular battlements, consisting of a parapet 1m high crowned with 60cm-high merlons. The total external height of the superstructure, therefore, was just shy of 8m.

2. The Aurelianic galleried curtain-wall. Some curtains contained galleries providing additional firing positions for archers. The curtain-wall was solid only to a height of about 3m, upon which base stood a low barrel-vaulted gallery supporting the rampart-walk and the battlements at the standard height.

3. The Aurelianic curtain-wall with Maxentian gallery above. The previous rampart-walk (1) was later covered with a vaulted gallery open on the interior with large arches and arrow-slits, each with a concave parapet, cut into the exterior. The new, second rampart-walk was open with battlements on the exterior. Archers manned the arcaded gallery, while *ballistae* were mounted on the crenellated open terrace above.

2

3

1

sharing a central, round-fronted tower that incorporated the massive tomb, minus its front. The latter was constructed like a bread store with a frieze illustrating the work in the occupant's bakeries.

The gateway at the head of the Pons Aelius was probably also of Type II, though almost nothing is known about it. Porta Aurelia-San Pancrazio, spanning the Via Aurelia Vetus on the crest of the Janiculum hill, may also belong to this category, though its demolition in 1643 to make way for the new fortifications of Pope Urbanus VIII has left insufficient evidence.

The third category (Type III: the Pinciana, Chiusa, Asinaria, Metrobia, Ardeatina and Septimiana gates) consisted of a single-span archway in the curtain-wall between two ordinary rectangular wall-towers at the usual interval. These gateways gave access to roads only used by local traffic. Devoid of flanking towers these gateways were originally scarcely more than posterns, though, as we shall see, several of them received more serious treatment in subsequent phases. Porta Pinciana on the north side of the city was an unusual example of a Type III. Offset in order to accommodate the oblique angle of the road passing through it, the Via Pinciana, the entranceway was apparently guarded by a single, rather narrow, round-fronted tower on the east side.

The fourth and final category (Type IV) encompasses the large number of anonymous posterns and doorways in Aurelian's wall, some of which probably served private needs. In addition to the small portal sometimes referred to as Porta Ostiensis West, four original posterns and two wickets are known in the wall. They were all similarly constructed, their narrow openings being surmounted by flat lintels and in two cases by flat arches, of travertine blocks. Above these door-heads were double relieving arches. Most, if not all, were blocked up at a very early date, probably under Maxentius (Richmond 1930: 219–21, 229–35, 247). Posterns, no fewer than five in number, also pierced the stretch of river wall from the Pons Agrippae up towards Porta Flaminia. These served the key ferry crossings and landing quays. Due to their commercial importance, these posterns remained open much longer than their landward counterparts.

The function of the wall

Aurelian obviously could not afford to leave Rome unguarded. Yet he could not afford to leave in Italy an army of sufficient size to guarantee the defence of Rome against a potential recurrence of the Germanic threat. He needed to muster as large an army as he could for his projected campaigns on the Danubian frontier and in the east. He also had to consider his own safety as emperor. His only option, therefore, was to build city walls behind which Rome could feel relatively secure from sudden attack.

Aurelian's campaign experience had shown him the value of urban fortifications to protect cities from northern barbarians not equipped with siege machines. Valerianus's defences around Thessalonica had enabled the city to hold out against the Goths until a relief army could reach it. Similarly, the defences with which Gallienus had enclosed Verona had allowed it to escape the ravages of the Alamanni. Of course the new defences had to be built at speed and with non-military labour and at a minimum cost, and, therefore, Aurelian's wall was austere rather than showy, serviceable rather than arresting. Only here and there, for example in the curtains of Type I gateways, was there any attempt at aesthetic embellishment.

It was clear from their structure and dimensions that the original fortifications were built to protect Rome from sudden attack by barbarian

invaders long enough for a relief force to be sent to the city's defence. These barbarians had no great expertise in siege warfare, an understandable failing among peoples who had no fortified cities of their own. What is more, they were slow to learn the techniques necessary for the building of siege machines, and even slower to develop the cohesion and deliberation needed to conduct a protracted siege (Thompson 1965: 131–40). The walls of Rome, therefore, were not designed to withstand concerted attack from an army equipped with sophisticated engines of war. The large number of entrances clearly demonstrates the truth of this. The point is underlined by the fact that so many of the posterns were closed and the remaining gateways strengthened when the military circumstances altered to increase the likelihood of siege warfare.

Certain tactical flaws in the design and construction of Aurelian's wall, which once again point to the lack of experience in this kind of construction on the part of the civilian workers involved, indicate that the function of the wall was as much a psychological deterrent as a physical barrier. These flaws are most obvious at those places where pre-existing structures have been incorporated. A glaring example is the total lack of communication along certain sections of the Aqua Claudia-Anio Novus around Porta Praenestina-Labicana and at the tenement house just to the north of this. The junction of the circuit with the north-west angle of the Castra Praetoria and the re-entrant east of Porta Ostiensis East also created unnecessary weak points (Richmond 1930: 67, 242–45, 248).

However, despite these apparent functional faults, the design of Aurelian's wall was clearly made with artillery defence in mind. The provision of windows in the gate- and wall-towers for the use of *ballistae* was a relatively innovative idea. This design further reinforces the anticipated nature of the attack the defences were intended to withstand. The artillery system had a limited range in the area directly in front of the wall itself, thus providing effective deterrence rather than meaningful defence. Nor was it possible to defend much more than a single sector of the circuit at any one time in this fashion.

The junction of Aurelian's wall with the north-west angle of Castra Praetoria, looking west-south-west in Viale del Policlinico towards Porta Nomentana. This was one of the weak points in the enceinte. (Author's collection)

1

2

3

4

1. The Aurelianic phase. A double-span archway faced with travertine is set in a two-storied curtain-wall. The twin portals are flanked by round-fronted towers covering the approaches to the gateway as well as enfilading the adjacent curtains. The gates themselves are of iron-bound oak. The first storey and the chamber above the entrance arches are pierced by round-headed windows. The second storey is an open terrace with battlements.

2. The Maxentian phase. Lofty, four-storied towers with rounded fronts, enclosing the original ones, have been added. These are 24m in height and 13m deep. The new galleried curtains now adjoin the gate-towers at the level of their third storey. In addition, a courtyard (not shown) has been constructed to the rear by running two walls in the form of pincers from the main gate. At the back of the new courtyard stands an archway associated with an earlier monument, a monumental arch of the Aqua Antoniniana,

and this has been utilized as the inner gate. From this courtyard staircases lead up to the new gate-towers.

3. The Honorian phase. The double-span archway has been reduced to a single portal. This reduction has been achieved by the insertion of a single-arched entranceway of re-used stone, one storey in height. The new entrance can be blocked with relative ease by means of a portcullis, a grille of wood lowered by ropes in a groove. Square bastions were built enclosing the round-fronted gate-towers up to the top of the intervening curtain-wall, the lower half being clad in re-used white marble.

4. The post-AD 442 phase. Following the major earthquake of AD 442, the gateway has undergone major structural repairs. These have been carried out by using courses of travertine blocks laid between bands of tile-facing. Despite the evidence of instability in this gateway, both gate-towers have been raised a storey.

To defend the city from all sides, as would be required in a formal siege, by arming every artillery emplacement would have required a complement of well over 700 *ballistae* in working order, together with the experienced military personnel to man them. It is highly unlikely that appreciable contingents of *ballistarii* were ever permanently stationed in Rome (Todd 1978: 34). Indeed, when faced with the serious prospect of a siege Honorius reverted instead to a primary reliance on archers, using artillery only as a reserve. Aurelian's wall thus represents 'a formidable barrier not a fighting platform' (Richmond 1930: 67).

A marble bust (Istanbul, Arkeoloji Müzesi) of Diocletianus (r. AD 284–305) from Nicomedia (Izmit). His military coup would mark the start of a new phase in Roman history. (Author's collection)

After Aurelian

The threat of barbarian invasion that prompted Aurelian to build his wall around Rome did not materialize. A measure of stability was created by perhaps the greatest of the Illyrian soldier-emperors, Diocletianus (r. AD 284–305), who gradually developed a system of power sharing known as the Tetrarchy. In its evolved form, there were two senior emperors, each known as Augustus, who ruled the eastern and western provinces respectively, assisted by a junior colleague or Caesar. In Diocletianus's view, and who are we to argue, the empire had grown too large and too complex to be governed by one man. This idea was nothing new.

Valerianus had divided the provinces on a geographical basis between himself and his son Gallienus, to whom he allotted the west. Yet Diocletianus's tetrarchic system went further. For not only was it designed to provide enough commanders to deal with several crises simultaneously, but by nominating the *Caesares* as successors to their senior colleagues it served to prevent civil war by providing for the ambitions of all men with armies. In time the two *Caesares* would became the new *Augusti* and appoint two new *Caesares* of their own. The Senate played no role in either the selection of emperors or the governance of the empire.

By AD 293 the system was up and running. Diocletianus and his co-emperor Maximianus, another Illyrian soldier, were the highest-ranking executives. Diocletianus reigned in the east, with Galerius as his Caesar; Maximianus controlled the west, with Constantius Chlorus as Caesar. The arrangements were sealed by dynastic marriages and the adoption of Diocletianus's family name Valerius, and widely advertised on coins and in official panegyric. Naturally, all four claimed the right to be worshipped as gods.

Then, without precedent, but probably with that natural human longing for the peace of retirement, Diocletianus abdicated his position (1 May AD 305). He felt that he had been in power long enough and there were ample safeguards to keep his new form of government in place. The restless old Maximianus, however, surrendered the purple only with extreme reluctance.

The walls of Rome now played an increasingly important military role, albeit against internal as opposed to external foes. In the successive refurbishments and strengthening that Aurelian's wall received, its function was altered to meet the new military climate, turning Rome into a fortress.

RIGHT
A marble bust (Paris, Musée du Louvre, MA3522 bis) of Maxentius (r. AD 306–12) from Langres. Self-styled *conservator urbis suae*, Maxentius carried out an assertive building programme, involving the curtains, towers and gateways, in a short space of time. (Esther Carré)

RIGHT
Pons Mulvius (Milvian Bridge), looking upstream from the west bank of the Tiber. This was the site of the decisive clash (28 October AD 312) between the western rivals, Constantinus and Maxentius. (Author's collection)

THE MAXENTIAN IMPROVEMENTS

Within a year of Diocletianus's lonely death the long expected rupture occurred in the west between the usurpers Constantinus (known to history as Constantine the Great), who ruled Gaul and Britannia, and Maxentius, the son of Diocletianus's former colleague Maximianus, who held Italy and had recently recovered Africa. The war was short and decisive. Forestalling his rival, Constantinus marched across the Alps and into Italy at great speed.

Having secured victory over Maxentius's northern forces near Augusta Taurinorum (Turin) and Verona, Constantinus marched on Rome. Maxentius opted to defend Rome, and accordingly cut the Pons Mulvius (Milvian Bridge), which carried the Via Flaminia across the Tiber, on the northern approach to the city. For some inexplicable reason he changed his mind, crossing the Tiber on a pontoon bridge moored just downstream of the now slighted stone bridge, and gave battle at Saxa Rubra, just a few kilometres north of the city walls (28 October AD 312).

Constantinus's army, although outnumbered, was battle-hardened and confident. Maxentius's army was thrown back in confusion and, as it retreated across the Tiber, the pontoon bridge collapsed. Maxentius and the Praetorian Guard were drowned in the swollen river, a scene flamboyantly depicted on the Arch of Constantine, the triumphal arch erected near the Colosseum in AD 315 to commemorate Constantinus's victory over his rival 'by the inspiration of the divinity' (*instinctu divinitatis*). The anxious Senate subserviently welcomed Constantinus as liberator of Rome and passively proclaimed him the sole emperor of the west. The Milvian Bridge would become one of the most famous battles in Roman history, mainly because of Constantinus's pronouncement afterwards that he owed his victory to the God of the Christians. There are three versions of this remarkable story.

It was some weeks prior to the battle, so he told his panegyrist Eusebius (*Vita Constantini* 1.28–29), bishop of Caesarea Palestinae, that he saw a sign

An exterior view of Porta Asinaria, looking north-north-west in Via Sannio, showing Maxentian rebuilding. Richmond suggests this gateway was distinguished in this monumental fashion because it lay on the road leading to the new Circus Maxentius. (Author's collection)

in the sky at midday, a cross of light superimposed on the sun. He took this as a sign of victory from the god whose symbol was the cross, stating under oath that he saw the words 'By this sign you will be victorious' (*Hoc signo victor eris*) written in stars around the cross. The night before the battle Christ appeared to him and instructed him to put this heavenly symbol on the standards of his army. He apparently did so with the desired results. Yet in a much earlier version of the same story (*Historia Ecclesia* 9.9), Eusebius does not mention any such vision, and is content to liken the victory, and in particular the engulfment of Maxentius's pagan troops in the Tiber, to the fate of Pharaoh's chariots at the crossing of the Red Sea.

According to the more credible version, that offered by Lactantius (*De mortibus persecutorum* 44.5–6), the night before the battle Constantinus dreamt that he was ordered to put the sign of Christ on the soldiers' shields. On awaking the next morning he put his faith to the test when he ordered his men to paint the *chi-rho* monogram (*XP*), the Greek initials of Christ superimposed, on their shields.

Whatever it was that happened to him before the battle, there is no doubt that Constantinus showed conspicuous favour to the Christians, then a vocal if small sect amongst many others, and continued to wear the symbol for Christ against every hostile power he faced. What is more, 'the New Rome which is the city of Constantinus', namely Constantinople, was formally dedicated by the emperor to the Holy Trinity and to the Mother of God (11 May AD 330).

The Maxentian curtains

Overall the curtains show two main phases of construction: the earlier comprises a solid wall in line with Aurelian's original scheme, the later a galleried structure, usually some 8m high, with a broad curtain-wall to the front and a continuous arcade on the inner side. This galleried wall is assigned to Maxentius's occupation of Rome (AD 306–12). Over the gallery ran a rampart-walk, a little more than 3m wide, fronted by a parapet and merlons.

LEFT
The Maxentian galleried wall along Viale Carlo Felice. Piercing the gallery curtain at irregular intervals are arrow-slits set in concave parapets. (Author's collection)

RIGHT
A tower in Viale Castrense, an exterior view looking west. Besides blocking up the round-headed windows, the Maxentian builders left this tower pretty much in its original, Aurelianic state. (Author's collection)

The walls of Rome, AD 312, showing the main roads into the city, aqueducts and key sites

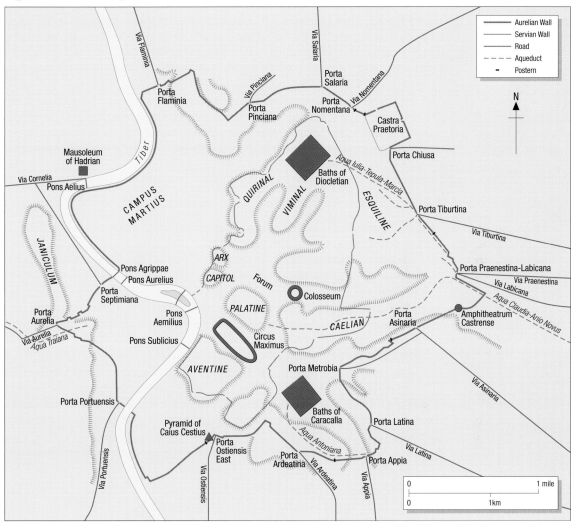

In the front face of the gallery, arrow-slits occurred at irregular intervals. The total height of the curtains from footings to merlons was now more than 15m, and in some places nearly 20m (Todd 1978: 49).

The construction process of the new work was broadly similar to that of the original structure, though the bricks and tiles used in the facing were not so scrupulously chosen and the bonding courses were omitted. This minor decline from the original higher standards is probably to be attributed to haste rather than to mere negligence or shoddy workmanship. Nevertheless, the overall standard of the work is still consistently high for so massive an undertaking.

As in the wall of the first period, the Maxentian work was not entirely uniform in construction throughout its entire length. One variant form existed in the south-west corner of the circuit, where the wall ran in front of the Aqua Claudia-Anio Novus. The Maxentian wall reached the level of the aqueduct and to support the new structure the Aurelianic curtains were extended to their rear and buttresses placed against the back of the heightened wall. The towers in this sector had been sited between the piers of the

The first milestone (Rome, Musei Capitolini, NCE3028) in Via Praenestina. The Latin inscription reads: 'To our Lord Maxentius Pius Fortunate Unconquered Augustus. First mile'. The repair of Italian roads was actively pursued during his short regime. (Esther Carré).

aqueduct so that access to the Maxentian wall could be had from these without the users climbing over or walking on the aqueduct channels. This unusually elaborate arrangement was thus a painstaking device to ensure that the flow of water in these two conduits was in no way interfered with.

Now that the wall had been raised considerably, the city possessed defences that only the most determined and prolonged siege could hope to penetrate. The galleried curtains meant that men and machines could be rushed to whatever sector required them. Furthermore, the enormous height of the upper rampart-walk gave not only improved vision to the defenders, but it also enabled a smaller number of them to engage and hold down an attacking group, thereby allowing greater flexibility of movement among those manning the wall. It is difficult to see how any ancient army could invest and take by siege operations an enceinte of this scale on a 19km circuit, and, as we shall see, the 'later history of Rome was to prove the truth of this and the worth of the wall of Aurelian and Maxentius' (Todd 1978: 50).

The Maxentian towers

The heightening of the curtains obviously brought changes to the towers, since they now rose to the level of the tower tops. But in the case of many of the towers, the resultant modifications were inconsiderable. In a number of surviving examples it is clear that the Maxentian workers left the Aurelianic towers much as they were, so that their crenellated open terraces projected forward of the wall at the same level as the new crenellated parapet.

Others, however, were substantially enlarged to take account of the new associated curtain-wall at the rear. In many, a large chamber covered by a hipped roof was built over the older open terrace, the parapet and merlons having been removed and the four windows below them blocked. These new upper chambers normally contained three round-headed windows in front, one to each side and two at the back, with a door giving access to the rampart-walk. In a small number of cases a more radical rebuilding was carried out. The old upper works were taken down to the level of the former

LEFT
A tower in Corso d'Italia, an exterior view looking south-east. Here the Maxentian builders have raised the tower one storey, and added new round-headed windows and a hipped roof. (Author's collection)

RIGHT
An exterior view of the east gate-tower of Porta Asinaria, looking north in Via Sannio, showing a rectangular Aurelianic tower and a Maxentian round-fronted addition. (Author's collection)

open terrace. Over this was then erected a new storey, covered like the other heightened towers with a hipped roof.

There are no discernible tactical or topographical reasons as to why the Maxentian workers gave such different treatments to the towers. As with the construction of the galleried wall, it may simply be a sign of haste. As Todd (1978: 52) points out, this ambitious scheme, begun probably in AD 307 when Rome was under threat, was still incomplete in AD 312 when Constantinus arrived from the north.

The Maxentian gateways

The second phase of construction affected two gateways in particular, the Appia and Asinaria. Two other gateways, the Latina and Ostiensis East, were modified on their internal faces but externally were hardly altered at all. In contrast, it was now that Porta Appia became the most splendid gateway of Rome, the Maxentian workmen having utterly transformed the strictly utilitarian gateway of Aurelian.

Porta Asinaria was originally a Type III until the major restoration work under Maxentius gave it a monumental appearance, with the addition of two large, round-fronted towers and the

Exterior view of Porta Pinciana, looking south in Piazza Brasile. The round-fronted tower on the right was built onto this Type III gateway under Maxentius. (Author's collection)

raising of the curtain-wall between. The Aurelianic entrance had been set, not quite centrally, between two rectangular wall-towers of which the southern example differed from the norm in having a staircase leading from the ground to the rampart-walk. The length of the curtain-wall between the towers is 30m and the entranceway only 4.5m so that the passage was barely adequately covered. The two wall-towers cannot be seen as flanking the gateway in any meaningful way and structurally they have nothing to do with it.

It was for this reason that the new round-fronted towers were added to those sides of the old rectangular wall-towers nearest to the entranceway, the new towers, and the old, being raised in four stories to a height of 18.5m. The curtain-wall between the towers rose almost to the level of the topmost storey. Porta Asinaria was clearly placed here to allow entry for the two roads approaching the city from the south-east, the Asinaria and Tusculana, but probably for economic reasons only a simple postern-type of entrance was provided. In the Maxentian rebuild economy was abandoned and Porta Asinaria was brought into line with the four great gateways while retaining its single entranceway.

None of the other gateways were distinguished in this monumental fashion. That Porta Appia should have been treated so comes as no surprise, since it spanned the consular road leading south. Todd (1978: 56) suggests that Maxentius intended most of the gateways to be enlarged in this manner

Towers

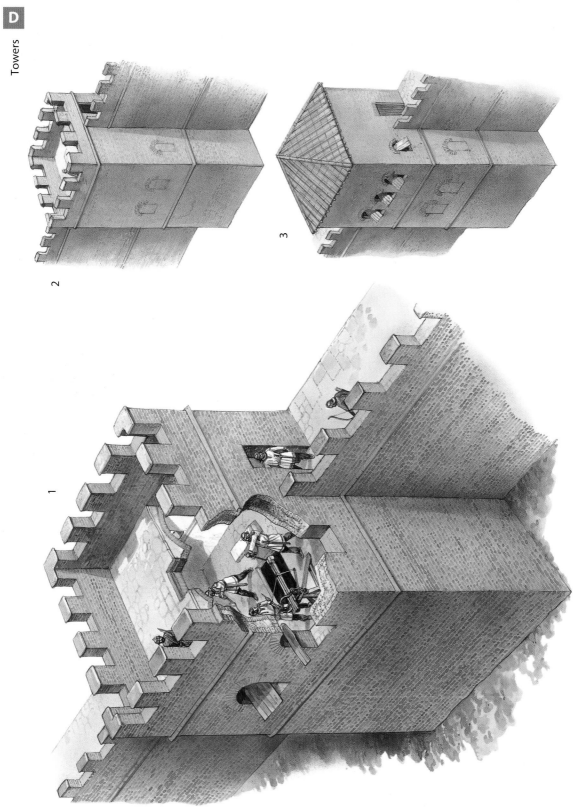

1

2

3

1. Aurelianic towers. Projecting towers, which now dominated enceintes, provided enfilading fire and advance positions for light artillery. The *ballista* was a two-armed torsion engine that fired bolts. With a range of some 400m, if used carefully, it could keep an enemy from coming in close to the defences. The towers themselves were uniformly rectangular in shape, measuring 7.6m across, projecting 3.35m in front of the curtain-wall and flushed with the back, and rising some 4.5m above the rampart-walk. This particular Aurelianic example has a triple, barrel-vaulted chamber with a central stairway leading up to its crenellated open terrace. The chamber is equipped with two round-headed windows facing forward for the use of its two *ballistae*, with another such window on either side to allow the machines to swivel 90 degrees.

2. In the first Maxentian example reconstructed here, the original parapet and merlons were removed and the four windows below them blocked. The builders then finished the modifications by simply raising the tower and adding a new crenellated open terrace.

3. In this more elaborate, second Maxentian example, a large chamber covered by a hipped roof has been built over the older open terrace, the parapet and merlons having been removed and the four windows below them blocked. The new upper chamber contains three round-headed windows in front, one to each side and two at the back, with a doorway allowing access to the new rampart-walk.

but events decided otherwise, thus forcing the builders to concentrate their efforts on the curtains and towers until Constantinus's victory brought Maxentius's programme (and his life) to a halt.

FROM HONORIUS TO BELISARIUS

On the death of Theodosius I (January AD 395), his elder son Arcadius, aged 18, took the east, while his brother Honorius, aged 11, became titular lord of the west. Honorius was pious and gentle, but incompetent and mulishly obstinate. The effective ruler of the west, and the outstanding military and political mind of his time, was the enigmatic generalissimo (*magister peditum praesentalis*) Stilicho. Half-Roman and half-Vandal, he had become Theodosius's chief lieutenant during the last years of his reign, and was married to his formidable niece (and adopted daughter) Serena. The dynastic connection of Stilicho and the imperial house was cemented by the marriage of his daughter Maria to Honorius, and when she died the emperor married her sister Thermantia.

A keystone (Rome, Museo delle Mura) with an incised Greek cross probably dating to the Honorian building phase, from an internal archway of Porta Appia. The Greek inscription reads: 'For the grace of God, to Saints Conone and George'. (Author's collection)

It was during the regency of Stilicho that Aurelian's wall was once again reorganized. This particular occasion was in the context of a large-scale incursion of Goths, the first time that invaders from the north had ranged widely in the Italian peninsula since Aurelian had faced the Iuthungi. With the passing away of Theodosius and the succeeding division of the empire, the Goths had taken the opportunity to relinquish their treaty with the empire. Six years later, Alaric, who exercised the leadership of what was effectively a mercenary army, decided to invade Italy, but was defeated by Stilicho, his former comrade-in-arms.

Stilicho was to fall to a palace coup and was beheaded (22 August AD 408). Honorius terminated his marriage and, it is said by Zosimus (5.35), 30,000 Germanic *foederati*, supporters of Stilicho, went over *en masse* to Alaric. The second invasion also ended in failure, but this time Alaric constrained the Senate in Rome to pay him a hefty endowment (November AD 408). Alaric blockaded Rome once more (late AD 409) to force Honorius, safe behind the walls and surrounding marshes of Ravenna, to give his followers land and annual payments of gold and corn. When negotiations broke down Alaric established a transient emperor, Priscus Attalus.

In the face of continued intransigence Alaric marched on Rome for a third time and broke in at Porta Salaria under the cover of darkness (24 August AD 410). The Goths plundered the city for three days but did comparatively little collateral damage. Alaric once more withdrew, this time heading south. He planned to cross to Africa, but died before this.

Honorius was momentarily aghast. The oddly domestic lifestyle he led in the remote but easily defensible Ravenna is illustrated, according to a bizarre anecdote of Procopius (*Wars* 3.2.25–26), by his reactions on being told Rome had perished. The emperor exclaimed in perplexity that it had just taken food from his hands. Matters were quickly explained to him and he sighed with relief: his enormous pet chicken, which was named 'Rome', was still in the very best of health.

The Honorian alterations

The alarm felt in Rome as Alaric's forces swept down the peninsula for the first time led those responsible for the city's defences to make still more formidable the already immensely strong fortifications. Even in what seemed at the time desperate circumstances, attention was paid to the appearance of the defences, especially the gateways, as well as their purely defensive capability. These changes were to be the last major work of an emperor on the walls of Rome.

According to the contemporary court-poet Claudian (*de VI Consulatu Honorii* 529–34) the building work began at the end of AD 401 when the first intelligence of Alaric's invasion reached Rome. This dating ties in nicely with three surviving building inscriptions (*CIL* 6.1188–90), the first, and indeed, only epigraphic records directly associated with the walls of Rome. The emergency was to last until Stilicho's victory at Pollentia (Pollenzo) on Easter Day AD 402 brought proof that Alaric could be stopped.

In fact little new work was carried out on the wall, the hurried programme being essentially one of repair and restoration. The curtains, despite their age, needed little attention, and the towers, too, were not greatly altered, beyond the replacement of windows by loopholes wherever this could be conveniently carried out. Once again it is the gateways in which the new mode makes it most striking impact.

Under Honorius Type I gateways, with the single exception of Porta Portuensis, were now reduced to a single entranceway some 4m in width, the façade being rebuilt in re-used stone, one storey high, and equipped with a portcullis. At the same time the gate-towers were incorporated within new

Belisarius's defence of Rome, 2 March AD 537–12 March AD 538

The defence of Rome was undoubtedly one of Belisarius's finest achievements, in which he managed to overcome all odds during a harrowing siege of one year and nine days. According to Procopius (*Wars* 5.22.17, 24.2), he initially had only a force of 5,000 men with which to man the extensive city walls.

On 2 March, having concluded a peace with the Franks so as to secure his rear, Vitigis arrived outside Rome with perhaps 50,000 men. He realized that to besiege the entire length of the wall effectively a huge force would be required, so he decided to build seven fortified camps mostly around the eastern perimeter, facing the gateways of the city. There was no attempt to construct any serious lines of circumvallation, and access into and out of the city was not entirely prevented.

On 21 March, the Ostrogothic attack began. Vitigis had constructed massive siege towers equipped with battering rams to be drawn by oxen up to the defences. Belisarius ordered his archers to ignore the assaulting troops and target the oxen. The towers halted well short of their goal. Only two Ostrogothic attacks ensued, but repeated fierce assaults had to be withstood.

The main one was directed against the Mausoleum of Hadrian and the defenders, once out of missiles, broke up the statues that surmounted the tomb, and pelted the attackers with lumps of marble until the assault failed. Meanwhile, a small force had found a weakness at the corner of the eastern defences, an old enclosure where wild animals had been kept prior to taking them to the Colosseum. Belisarius relieved the pressure of the attacks by launching sorties from other gateways. Vitigis decided to starve the city.

The monotony was interrupted by occasional imperial sallies that inflicted serious damage on the Ostrogoths. A number of large-scale encounters were fought outside the city walls too, in which sometimes one side, sometimes the other, came off best. Vitigis, for his part, had the trans-Tibertine aqueducts destroyed, hoping to halt production in the flour mills. Belisarius simply began using the Tiber to keep the mill wheels turning. Nevertheless, what little supply of food that was trickling in from outside soon dried up once Vitigis had seized the port of Rome.

The Ostrogoths, however, were also suffering from hunger and disease, and their advantages were beginning to melt away. In November a new body of imperial reinforcements, which would double Belisarius's forces, landed in Italy together with extensive provisions. The Ostrogoths tried to block their arrival, and this failure cast grave doubts on Vitigis's chances of success before Rome. He began to negotiate, and a three-month truce was granted so that Ostrogothic envoys could go to Constantinople to speak with Iustinianus. Belisarius used the time to strengthen his position and make some moves to the north. When the truce was broken by Ostrogothic attempts to force an entry into Rome via the aqueducts, Belisarius retaliated by raiding behind Vitigis's lines. Now in despair, Vitigis retreated to Ravenna.

towers of rectangular plan and built of re-used stone. The combined effect of the Honorian towers and the stone curtains was not only to strengthen but also to enhance the external appearance of these major gateways.

Other gateways were also included in this work of blocking. Porta Tiburtina, originally a monumental arch carrying the Aqua Iulia-Tepula-Marcia over Via Tiburtina, had its entranceway reduced to a similar width of 4m, while Porta Asinaria was blocked altogether by brickwork, never to be reopened. Porta Chiusa, which had been narrowed by Maxentius to only 3.6m, was now also entirely blocked and never again re-used. All the surviving single-portal gateways, and several of those now vanished, were provided with curtains in travertine.

LEFT
Under Honorius the double-portalled Porta Ostiensis East was reduced to a single portal. This was effected by the insertion of a one-storey curtain of travertine provided, as made manifest by the slot shown here, with a portcullis. (Author's collection)

RIGHT
An exterior view of Porta Tiburtina, looking south-east in Via Tiburtina Antica, showing the Honorian alterations. Its portal was reduced in width by the insertion of a well-constructed travertine gate-house. (Author's collection)

Aurelian's wall at Porta Ostiensis East, c. AD 400

The walls of Rome represent at once both the most emblematic and the most enduring of Aurelianic monuments. Indeed nothing else so eloquently demonstrates that, by Aurelian's day, the empire was now on the back foot. The wall itself was a massive obstacle, comprising 19km of brick-faced concrete nearly 3.7m thick and 8m high (rising to more than 15m after the reorganization of Maxentius), with 381 enfilading towers and 18 gateways.

This scene, set during the reign of Honorius (AD 395–423), illustrates a stretch of the wall from the Tiber to Porta Ostiensis East. The gateway itself has been modified as part of the emperor's recent programme of repair and restoration, whereby all the double-portalled gateways on the main roads, bar one, have been reduced to a single entranceway. As we witness with Porta Ostiensis East, this reduction was achieved by the insertion of a curtain of re-used stone, one storey in height and pierced by a single-arch portal equipped with a portcullis. Just to the west of the gateway stands the famous Pyramid of Caius Cestius. This imposing funerary monument was already of respectable antiquity at the time it was embodied into the fabric of the wall back in AD 271.

Some of the gateways were afforded somewhat different treatment. At Porta Ostiensis East the new-style facing was applied but to the old round-fronted towers. An extra storey was also added here. Two gateways, the Salaria and Nomentana, were not given new facings in stone at all, thought the first was heightened by an extra storey, as was Porta Pinciana.

The ceremonial character of the Honorian treatment of the gateways was further emphasized, in some cases at least, by the handsome inscriptions on their new stone-faced curtains. As already mentioned, three instances are known, of which one (*CIL* 6.1190), on Porta Tiburtina, remains *in situ*, and another (*CIL* 6.1189), from Porta Praenestina-Labicana, survives in part and has been reconstructed at the site of the gateway (Todd 1978: 61, 63–64).

The Belisarian alterations

Behind its massive city walls, Rome remained a vigorous and lively place. There has been a tendency to assume that after Alaric's success the *urbs aeterna* was semi-ruinous, drear and beggarly. There is no justification for this view. Apart from some material damage, the actual result of the 'sack of Rome' was a great loss of prestige and shock. The very presence of its strong defences meant that a civilized and prosperous life could go on. Although signs of depopulation and decay were already visible, for Procopius 6th-century Rome remained 'the grandest and most noteworthy of all cities under the sun' (*Wars* 7.22.9). Despite the hyperbole, the name of old Rome still had power, and in Constantinople, the New Rome, the eastern emperor Iustinianus (Justinian, r. AD 527–65) longed to re-establish single control over the old empire and its capital.

Iustinianus certainly possessed the necessary military resources, albeit only on one front at a time, and ambition to accomplish this, but was determined to do so cheaply. Luckily for him he had the services of one of the most talented of imperial generals, Belisarius, who was placed in command of an expeditionary force of 15,000 imperial troops and 1,000 foreign auxiliaries. He also had the services of some 1,100 *bucellarii* or, as Procopius appropriately describes them, 'those who stand behind when the commander is dining' (*Wars* 4.28), and horse-warriors, including 300 Huns, who had given a personal oath of allegiance to Belisarius.

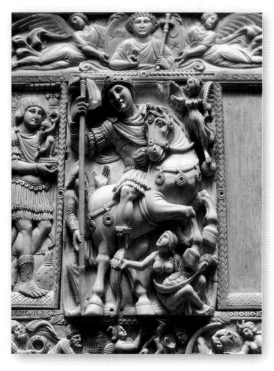

An ivory diptych (Paris, Musée du Louvre OA9063), c. AD 532, known as the 'Barberini Ivory'. The horseman probably represents a triumphant Iustinianus I (r. AD 527–65), whose grand ambitions included the recovery of Italy. (Esther Carré)

A late 5th-century mosaic (Ravenna, Palace of Theodoric, Portico A frs. 4–6), depicting an Ostrogothic horseman hunting a wild boar. In battle light spears were the primary Ostrogoth weapon, with iron swords, of the long-bladed double-edged Sassanid type, serving as a secondary weapon. (Author's collection)

Having conquered Vandal Africa in a lightning campaign, Belisarius, with just 7,500 regulars and his indispensable *bucellarii*, took Ostrogothic Sicily (AD 535) then Naples by siege and Rome by negotiation (AD 536). Successfully defending Rome for a year against Vitigis (r. AD 536–40), Belisarius next fought his way up the peninsula and occupied the former imperial capital of Ravenna (AD 540).

The rapid conquest, however, was only superficial. The weak and divided Ostrogothic leadership had contributed much to Belisarius's spectacular success, and with the emergence of an energetic and able leader in Totila (r. AD 541–52) the military balance swung back in favour of the Ostrogoths. From the main Ostrogothic settlements north of the Po, Totila quickly re-conquered Italy and Sicily, except for a few coastal strongholds. Moreover, Persian attacks on the empire meant the imperial army in Italy was starved of men and *matériel*. Worse still, the army lost Belisarius, who was recalled to command on the eastern front.

Prior to the arrival of Belisarius, the alterations to Aurelian's wall were matters of repair and refurbishing rather than major reconstruction. After the earthquake of AD 442 large cracks appeared in the southern sector of the wall between the Appia and Metrobia gates. Porta Appia itself was affected by the earthquake and required large-scale repairs. Certain parts of the city walls were now given buttresses, notably to the east of Porta Latina and of Porta Appia.

Against the threat of the returning Ostrogoths Belisarius reconstructed those parts of the city walls that had suffered damage or decay, equipping each merlon of the battlements with a spur wall so as to cover the exposed left side of defenders from missile fire, a defensive device not hitherto used on Aurelian's wall. Drafting local workers, he also dug a ditch or ditches around the city, of which no trace now survives. In front of some of the gateways large man-traps were set. Known as wolves (*lupi*), these were a form of spiked drawbridge that were designed to be dropped on assaulting troops. As the aqueducts of the city could also provide a means of entry for the enemy, Belisarius had them sealed off by filling their channels with masonry for a considerable distance. All this is told by Procopius (*Wars* 5.14.15, 19.18, 21.19–22). He was present during the Ostrogothic siege of Rome, being a civil servant who served in a logistical capacity on the staff of Belisarius.

Procopius, a civilian who obviously had an eye for military affairs, also tells us (*Wars* 5.21.14, 18) that bolt-shooting *ballistae* were installed in the towers and that stone-throwing *onagri* were mounted on the curtains. A bolt-shooter fired large body-piercing bolts (*iaculi*), whereas a stone-thrower simply relied on the weight of its projectile to crush the target. Both machines were an important factor in the successful defence of Rome, playing havoc with the Ostrogothic machinery, which was in any case held at some distance from the wall by the new ditch-system, and serving as effective anti-personnel weapons. Procopius says (*Wars* 5.23.9–11) that a lone Ostrogothic archer was shot by a bolt from an engine mounted on a tower, the missile passing through his cuirass and body, pinning him firmly to the tree he was standing next to.

After Vitigis withdrew, further repairs took place before Rome once again came under threat. An Ostrogothic force under Totila was by treachery allowed to break into the city at Porta Asinaria (17 December AD 545). The king, recognizing the immense strength of the wall, set about demolishing large stretches of it, but did not proceed far with the work before Belisarius, who was now back in Italy, recovered Rome in the following spring. The damage caused by Totila's men was restored, and some of these repairs can still be seen in the facing of the curtains, where re-used blocks of travertine and marble have been thrust into the gashed fabric. At the towers, a botching job was carried out, the stone blocks being simply pushed up against the earlier facing to form a rudimentary buttress. Nevertheless, when Totila again invested Rome (summer AD 548), the battered old city held out surprisingly well.

AURELIAN'S LEGACY

The cities of Ostrogothic Italy, in general, had suffered devastation from siege and counter-siege in Iustinianus's opportunistic war of re-conquest (AD 536–54), and the Rome that Procopius had once visited had likewise suffered grievously from the interminable hostilities. Paradoxically, the emperor's attempt to bring back Roman rule to Rome did more damage than the barbarian visitations the city had endured so far. The heavy reliance on the strategy of blockade

An angle-tower in Via Casilina, in an exterior view looking west. Belisarian restoration work is easily recognized when re-used blocks of travertine and marble have been thrust into the gashed fabric of the city walls. (Author's collection)

meant that some sieges were protracted and Rome, as we have seen, twice underwent lengthy investments of a year's duration in the space of a decade.

Behind the city walls the population had already shrunk from around 800,000 in Maxentius's time to perhaps 80,000 under the Ostrogothic kings, most of them concentrated in the west of the city near the bend of the Tiber, from the foot of the Palatine and the Capitol down to the river and on the west bank in the Janiculum quarter. Many of the old senatorial families had already died out. The Gothic war then ruined many of the families that survived, who abandoned their urban villas and rural estates and took refuge in the eastern empire.

Around its dwindling population, meanwhile, the physical city decayed. The ancient city prefect (*praefectus urbi*) still held office under the Ostrogothic kings and after the Gothic war, and under him were officials in charge of building maintenance and restoration as well as dedicated funds for purchasing the necessary bricks and mortar. Procopius found the Romans to be 'lovers of their city' (*philopolides*) beyond all others and noted that during the previous Ostrogothic regime 'they had mostly preserved the city's buildings and their adornments even though under barbarian rule' (*Wars* 4.22.5–6). The new construction mostly comprised churches.

The Papacy presided over a building programme that left most of the Augustan regions shimmering with spacious new basilicas. The popes themselves bore most of the cost, as they had the necessary means. As the senatorial aristocracy abandoned Rome and central Italy they bequeathed their cherished estates to the see of Rome, which became the greatest landowner in the peninsula and in Sicily as well. With these buildings each pontiff impressed his stamp on Rome, as its secular as well as its spiritual ruler. As such they also frequently managed secular urban construction. By the time of Gregory the Great (AD 590–604), stability and a level of prosperity had returned, and Rome had taken on its medieval dress.

The *trace italienne*

The invasion of Italy in the winter of 1494 by Charles VIII of France soon demonstrated that the medieval fortifications of Europe were now redundant. With astonishing speed Charles had taken, one after another, castles and fortified cities, all of which had crumbled before the pounding of his 40 or so gleaming bronze guns discharging wrought-iron balls. Francesco Guicciardini, a contemporary diplomat and historian, wrote that the cannon were 'planted against the walls of a town with such speed, the space between shots was so little, and the balls flew so quick and were impelled with such force, that as much execution was done in a few hours as formerly, in Italy, in the like number of days' (quoted in Parker 1996: 10). This was no exaggeration. In February of 1495 the French attacked the Neapolitan citadel of Monte San Giovanni, a fortress that had earlier withstood a siege of seven years. The cannon opened a breach in four hours. According to another witness to these fiery events, Guicciardini's fellow Florentine Niccolò Machiavelli, 'the force of artillery is such that no wall can stand, not even the thickness, for more than a few days' (*Discourses* 2.17). And so with this revolution in siege warfare the empirical knowledge of the builder and the soldier about fortifying a site no longer sufficed.

Hitherto, the strength of a fortress had derived principally from the height of its walls: the higher the wall the more difficult for the storming-party to scale

An exterior view of Porta Flaminia, looking south-south-east at the junction of Piazzale Flaminio and Via Flaminio. Its present state, apart from the side arches (1877), represents the gateway erected for Pope Pius IV Medici (1559–65). It is now known as Porta del Popolo. (Author's collection)

F BELISARIUS'S DEFENCE OF ROME

The citizens of Rome had submitted to Belisarius in the first place to avoid a siege at his hands, and were thus hardly disposed to endure one patiently under him. They soon became dissatisfied with the conditions, being unable to bathe, badly provisioned, and obliged to forgo sleep in guarding the city walls. In response, which was also in part a solution for his chronic lack of manpower, Belisarius mingled his soldiers and able-bodied civilians together and distributed them to different places, setting a fixed daily wage for the services of these Roman 'volunteers' – or so says one member of the general's retinue, Procopius (*Wars* 5.25.11).

In this scene we see lightly equipped archers, which formed the bulk of Belisarius's infantry force, manning the city walls. Mingled with them are the newly raised citizen-archers. The principal weapon of the professional shooters is the composite bow with short, powerful limbs. The quiver, slung from a strap across the left shoulder, carries 40 arrows. Their secondary weapon is a light battleaxe employed in conjunction with a small parrying shield, which is normally hung at their belts. The civilians, on the other hand, are armed with an assortment of self bows and side arms, many of the latter domestic in origin. Meantime, outside the city walls Belisarius leads his horsemen in yet another sortie against the besieging Ostrogoths.

The Bastione del Sangallo (1538–42), an exterior view looking west in Viale di Porta Ardeatina. Quadrilateral, angled bastions were designed to resist artillery bombardment rather than human assault; the age of 'vertical defence' had passed. (Author's collection)

A splayed embrasure (above) and a vaulted casemate (below) at the Bastione del Sangallo. Built squat and solid, two of its sides pointed outwards and carried heavy artillery, while the other two stood at right angles to the main wall and bristled with anti-personnel weapons. (Author's collection)

the crest, while the thickness entailed by height rendered attack by siege engines less effective. Counter-weighted machines (tension artillery) threw projectiles that struck only glancing blows at such walls; spring-powered machines (torsion artillery), though working with a flat trajectory, were intrinsically under-powered. Even stone-firing bombards had made little impression upon the art of siege warfare. The only certain means of bringing down a wall was to attack it at its base by mining, a laborious task that ditches and moats readily defeated, and that was also open to the riposte of counter-mining.

The new cannon could be brought rapidly into action close to a wall, and then handled to fire accurately in a predictable arc of impact; their advent effectively transferred the effect of mining to combustible artillery. Compact iron cannonballs, directed at the base of a wall in a horizontal pattern of attack that did not vary in height, rapidly cut a channel in the stonework. The cumulative effect was to use the physics of the wall against itself: the higher the wall, the more quickly it would become unstable and the wider the breach it left when it toppled.

French powder makers and gun casters had reshaped the slow-firing and very immobile bombard into an efficient prototype of the modern gun. Lighter, more manoeuvrable cannons firing an energetic new form of powder created a destructive weapons system. And so with relative ease Charles's state-of-the-art cannon had knocked down walls that had stood stoutly for many centuries, thereby making good his claim to the Kingdom of Naples.

Italy, appalled at the easiness of the trans-Alpine king's triumphal march to Naples, would soon become the new school of not only experienced master masons, but also experts in mathematics and engineering. It was Giuliano da Sangallo, with his brother Antonio, who founded the first and most important of the Italian fortification 'families', an extremely competitive group of Mafia-like bands that were contained by ties of blood, companionship and patronage. These not only included the Sanmicheli, Savorgnano, Peruzzi, Genga and Antonelli, but also such unlikely practitioners as Leonardo da Vinci, who, in spite of his conviction that war was *bestialissima pazzia*, became inspector of fortresses to Cesare Borgia (1502), and Buonarroti Michelangelo, who, as Commissary General of Fortifications, equipped his native Florence with new defences (1527–29).

The Bastion in Viale Aurelio Saffi, erected under Pope Urbanus VIII (1643), equipped with gun-ports and loops. Guns of all calibres could be either fired over the parapet, or concealed and fired through embrasures cut into the parapet. (Author's collection)

Michelangelo, who is now remembered chiefly for his titanic struggles with blocks of marble and the ceiling of the Sistine Chapel, was also renowned in his own day as a military engineer. In 1545, in a course of a heated argument with Antonio da Sangallo minor, the renowned military architect employed by the Farnese family, he gave vent to the astonishing statement that 'I do not know very much about painting and sculpture, but I have gained a great experience of fortifications, and I have already proved that I know more about them than you and the whole tribe of the Sangallos' (Clausse 1901: 2.351).

It was Antonio da Sangallo minor who had been hired by the Pope to add 18 powerful bastions to Aurelian's wall in addition to five for the defence of the Vatican (1538–42). Those that were erected were done so along the southern sector of the wall, an area of Rome most vulnerable to attack. The Bastione del Sangallo, near Porta Ardeatina, probably represents the acme of 16th-century Italian military architecture. The cost, however, was astronomical. The scheme to surround Rome with a belt of bastions was abandoned when the construction of this one bastion alone was found to have cost 44,000 ducats (Parker 1996: 12).

As high walls were extremely vulnerable to the law of ballistics, new walls to resist the cannon therefore needed to stand low. However, a fortress so built was open to escalade, the rushing forward of a storming-party with ladders to sweep over the crest and into the fortress interior by surprise attack. The new system of fortification had to incorporate features that resisted bombardment and, at the same time, held the enemy's foot soldiers at bay. The solution to this problem of surrendering height while acquiring depth was the solid angular bastion. Strong enough not to be battered shapeless by a concentration of enemy fire, this wall-high structure stood well forward of the main wall, where it dominated the ditch or moat, and served as a firing platform for gunpowder weapons.

The most suitable design proved to have four faces. Two of these formed a wedge that pointed out toward the surrounding countryside so as to present a glancing surface to enemy fire, and where big ordnance could be mounted to fire out across the glacis. The other two faces, those that joined the wedge to the main wall at right angles, from the ramparts of which defenders could use small-calibre firearms, both hand-held and mounted, served to sweep the ditch and stretches of curtain between bastions. The bastions should be built of stone, though brick was an acceptable substitute, backed and filled with

A bronze equestrian statue of Garibaldi (1807–82), Piazza Gramsci, Siena. It was 'his fortune never to take full part in the common prose life of civilised men', wrote George Macaulay Trevelyan. (Author's collection)

rammed earth to better absorb the shock of shot, the whole constituting a structure of immense solidity so as to provide both a rock-solid cannon platform and a sloping outer face on which impacting shot would make the least possible impression.

The German artist Albrecht Dürer, having studied in Italy, took the blueprint for this style of gunpowder fortifications north. He published the first treatise on the new defensive system, which spread across Europe under the name *trace italienne*. Over a period of 50 years the quintessential bastion neutralized many of the advantages of improved cannon and returned siege warfare to a new equilibrium. The *trace italienne* would develop into the fearful geometry of fortification associated with the most famous of French military engineers, Vauban.

Garibaldi's Rome

In February 1849, some 19 centuries after its demise, the Roman Republic was revived. In France the ambitious new president of the Second Republic, Louis-Napoléon Bonaparte (before long Napoléon III, Emperor of the French), dispatched an army to restore the Pope and 'liberate' Rome from the handful of dangerous radicals who, as he saw it, had forced themselves

G GARIBALDI'S DEFENCE OF ROME

Throughout the medieval and early modern periods, Aurelian's wall was maintained and added to, chiefly by the Papacy. The last occasion on which the wall proved a significant factor in military affairs was in the mid 19th century, when Garibaldi managed for some time to hold off the French.

Porta San Pancrazio was erected during the pontificate of Pope Urbanus VIII, towards the end of the Thirty Years War, on the site of Porta Aurelia. It was the key gateway of the new anti-ballistic walls built to protect the Janiculum and the Vatican from attacks coming from the sea. It was the stretch of curtains and bastions near Porta San Pancrazio, re-created here in this scene, which was defended by Garibaldi and his volunteer Italian Legion of 1,300 men. Every morning, according to his memoirs, Garibaldi stood on the ramparts

and there, unhurriedly, he lit his first cigar of the day while French sharpshooters filled the air around him with lead. In the foreground, waiting attentively, stands Garibaldi's batman, the black Brazilian Andrea Aguiar, who has been his constant companion since his exploits in South America. The Garibaldini emulated their leader, who addressed them as the 'sons of heroism' and encouraged them to conduct themselves as a privileged elite. Their flowing locks and tremendous moustaches, sweeping capes and broad plumed hats, their belts stuck with daggers and pistols were conspicuous symbols of their pride and swagger. Yet it was the distinctive dress of the Garibaldini, the red shirts, which were to become famous all over the world and prized as relics long after their wearers were dead.

A manikin (Marsala, Museo Civico) dressed as a Garibaldino at the time of the defence of Rome. The idiosyncratic shirt had evolved, six years earlier, out of a requisitioned stock of bright red overalls destined for slaughterhouse workers. (Author's collection)

upon the unwilling citizens. On 27 April Garibaldi led his followers into Rome through streets packed with people shouting his name. He entered the city riding a white horse and wearing a black slouch hat and a swirling white poncho, which was flung back to show his celebrated red shirt. Behind him clattered his 'brigand-band' of red-shirted followers, the Garibaldini. The Roman commander was General Avezzana, and of the nearly 20,000 men under his command, the Garibaldini constituted only a small fraction. But Giuseppe Garibaldi (1807–82) is remembered as the defender of the brief Roman Republic.

On 29 April, with Avezzana's approval, Garibaldi occupied the Villa Corsini, a private house set in gardens just outside and perched on a hill above the western sector of the city walls. The following day the French marched lackadaisically up to Rome's Janiculum quarter, assured by the reports of an easy entrance into the city. Garibaldi sent his men, seasoned Garibaldini and new Roman recruits alike, racing downhill to repulse them. Initially the French held their ground, but when Garibaldi personally led a second charge, they turned and fled. A French representative negotiated a cease-fire that allowed the French army to remain *in situ* as a shield against an Austrian (Hapsburg) army poised to the north, or so the Romans were told.

Meanwhile, the army of the Bourbon king of Naples was menacing Rome from the south. Garibaldi went to meet it under the command of Colonel Pietro Roselli. There was a desperate, inconclusive engagement at Velletri, where Garibaldi came close to being killed: he and his horse were thrown down and badly trampled by some of his own retreating horsemen. Having been dragged clear of a tangled heap of fallen horses and men, he returned to Rome with his battered band.

On 1 June the French general Charles Oudinot, his army now heavy reinforced, gave notice that he was ending the armistice. The Romans, understanding themselves to have three days to prepare, were taken completely by surprise when, on 2 June, the French, determined not to be beaten, occupied the undefended Villa Corsini. Garibaldi was given the task of recapturing it.

The battle for Villa Corsini, which took place on 3 June, was a terrible one. For 17 hours, from dawn to dusk on a sweltering hot day, Garibaldi sent wave after wave of men up the rising ground between the city walls and the villa, through its narrow garden gate and up the steeply sloping drive towards the front of the four-storey villa, where from every window, balcony and terrace the French were firing on them. Twice the villa was taken 'at the point of the bayonet', but each time the French, who could approach it under the cover of trees to the rear, swiftly retook it. With the French immovably entrenched in the hilltop villa the fall of Rome was inevitable.

For another month the Republic held out. Garibaldi commanded the defence of the most desperately beleaguered section of the city walls. On the night of 29 June the French, having completed their siege lines, launched the final offensive. For two hours Garibaldi valiantly led the defenders as they struggled to hold back the assault. At last, as the western sector collapsed under the French bombardment and the invaders came pouring through the breach, Garibaldi rode over the Tiber to the Capitol where the Assembly was in session. Rome was lost and the great political experiment had failed. But when he walked into the chamber covered in blood, sweat and dust, the Assembly rose as one man and cheered him. The republican government surrendered, but Garibaldi, fated to become Europe's greatest republicans, did not.

THE SITES TODAY

The traveller to Rome today can still see a good percentage of Aurelian's wall and with four days to spare he or she will be able to examine all the remains at leisure and in some detail. Starting at Porta Pinciana, on the north side of the circuit, and following Corso d'Italia to Porta Nomentana (now Porta Pia), good stretches of the wall, still complete with roofed towers, can be studied. This first day ends at the Castra Praetoria, whose defences were heightened and incorporated into the Aurelianic circuit.

The Servian wall, at Stazione Centrale Roma Termini. Despite its incongruous *mise en scène* at a McDonald's restaurant, the short stretch of wall here can be studied at close-quarters. (Author's collection)

The second day picks up the wall again at the Castra Praetoria and the walk continues south of the camp to where the railway tracks out of Stazione Roma Centrale Termini slice through the line of the defences. For this section take either Viale Pretoriano (inside the wall) or Viale di Porta Tiburtina (outside the wall) to Porta Tiburtina. From the gateway follow Via di Porta Labicana – note the blocked postern opposite Via dei Marsi – and finish the day at Porta Praenestina-Labicana (now Porta Maggiore).

The third day starts at the Amphitheatrum Castrense, hard by the junction of Viale Castrense with Via Nola, and follows the south side of the circuit past the Asinaria, Metrobia (now Porta Metronia), Latina and Appia (now Porta San Sebastiano) gates. This is the most rewarding sector of the wall, and a must for those with only a day to spare.

The fourth day starts back at Porta Appia, which houses the small but excellent Museo delle Mura (Via di Porta San Sebastiano 18), and continues eastward along Viale di Porta Ardeatina, pass Porta Ardeatina, to Porta Ostiensis East (now Porta San Paolo) and the Pyramid of Caius Cestius. Again, the wall along this sector is well worth seeing and includes the beautifully built Bastione del Sangallo.

There are, of course, one or two other places associated with the city walls that can be visited. By crossing the Tiber to Trastevere by the Ponte Sublicio, for instance, and making one's way to Villa Sciarra, the gunpowder fortifications of Pope Urbanus VIII can be explored. It was on this western sector of the city walls that the Garibaldini valiantly held out against the

French. Further up the river and just beyond the Vatican is the papal fortress of Castel Sant'Angelo, part of which is the mausoleum that Hadrian himself designed, its massive drum being later incorporated into the city's defences.

Another location worth visiting is Stazione Roma Centrale Termini. Between the railway station and the Museo Nazionale Romano, in Piazza dei Cinquento, stands the best-preserved section of the so-called Servian wall. Beneath the station itself, surrounded by the chairs and tables of McDonald's, two very short sections of this wall can be closely examined too.

GLOSSARY AND ABBREVIATIONS

Augustus	Imperial title designating the two senior members of the Tetrarchy.
Ballista/ballistae	Light, twin-armed torsion engine firing bolts.
Ballistarii	Specialist *ballista* (q.v.) operators.
Bonding courses	Horizontal courses of stone, brick or re-used tile built at vertical intervals up the wall in order to tie in the shallow facing into the mass of the core.
Bucellarii	'Biscuits-eaters' – armed retainers of a Roman commander.
Caesar	Imperial title designating the two junior members of the Tetrarchy.
Foederati	Barbarians, under ethnic leaders, serving a Roman emperor.
Header	A stone block placed lengthways from front to rear across a wall so that its end is flush with the outer surface (cf. stretcher).
Iaculum/iaculi	*Ballista* bolt.
Mille passus/ milia passuum	'One-thousand paces' – a Roman mile (1,618 yards/1.48km).
Onager/onagri	'Wild ass' – a single-armed torsion engine throwing stones.
Parapet	A low narrow defensive wall, usually with crenels (open part) and merlons (closed part), along the upper outer edge of the curtains.
Pozzolana	Volcanic sand giving strength when mixed in cement.
Stretcher	Stone block placed horizontally with its length parallel to the length of a wall (cf. header).
Travertine	Grey-white stone suitable and popular for building both in the Roman period and today.
Tufa	A porous rock formed of calcium carbonate (chalk) deposited from springs.

Abbreviations

CIL T. Mommsen *et al.*, *Corpus Inscriptionum Latinarum* (Berlin, 1862–)
ILS H. Dessau, *Inscriptiones Latinae Selectae* (Berlin, 1892–1916)
PBSR *Proceedings of the British School at Rome*
SHA *Scriptores Historiae Augustae* (London, 1932)
TAPA *Transactions of the American Philological Association*
Wars Procopius, *History of the Wars* (London, 1919)

BIBLIOGRAPHY

Barker, J.W. *Justinian and the Later Roman Empire* (London: University of Wisconsin Press, 1966)

de Blois, L. *The Policy of the Emperor Gallienus* (Leiden: E.J. Brill, 1976)

Downey, G. 'Aurelian's victory over Zenobia at Immae, AD 272', *TAPA* 81: pp. 57–68 (1950)

Elton, H. *Warfare in Roman Europe, AD 350–425* (Oxford: Clarendon Press, 1996, 1997)

Heather, P.J. *The Goths* (Oxford: Clarendon Press, 1996)

Hughes-Hallett, L. *Heroes: Saviours, Traitors and Supermen* (London: Fourth Estate, chapter 7, 2004)

Jones, A.H.M. *The Later Roman Empire: a Social, Economic and Administrative Survey*, 2 vols (Oxford: Clarendon Press, 1964)

Marsden, E.W. *Greek and Roman Artillery: Historical Development* (Oxford: Clarendon Press, 1969)

Marsden, E.W. *Greek and Roman Artillery: Technical Treatises* (Oxford: Clarendon Press, 1971)

Osier, J. 'The emergence of the third century equestrian military commanders' *Latomus* 36: pp. 674–87 (1977)

Parker, G. *The Military Revolution: Military Innovation and the Rise of the West, 1500–1800*, 2nd edition (Cambridge: Cambridge University Press, 1996)

Rankov, N.B. *The Praetorian Guard*, Elite series no. 50 (Oxford: Osprey Publishing, 1994)

Richardson, L. *A New Topographical Dictionary of Ancient Rome* (Baltimore: Johns Hopkins University Press, 1992)

Richmond, I.A. 'The relation of the Praetorian Camp to Aurelian's Wall of Rome', *PBSR* 10: pp. 12–22 (1927)

Richmond, I.A. *The City Walls of Imperial Rome: An Account of its Architectural Development from Aurelian to Narses* (Oxford: Clarendon Press, 1930)

Rostovtzeff, M.I. *Social and Economic History of the Roman Empire*, 2nd edition (Oxford: Clarendon Press, 1957)

Saunders, R.T. *A Biography of the Emperor Aurelian, AD 270–275*, Ph.D. dissertation (University of Cincinnati, 1991)

Southern, P. *The Roman Empire from Severus to Constantine* (London: Routledge, 2001)

Southern, P. and K.R. Dixon *The Late Roman Army* (London: Routledge, 1996, 2000)

Stoneman, R. *Palmyra and its Empire: Zenobia's Revolt against Rome* (Ann Arbor: University of Michigan Press, 1992)

Thompson, E.A. *The Early Germans* (Oxford: Clarendon Press, 1965)

Todd, M. *The Walls of Rome* (London: Elek Books, 1978)

Todd, M. *The Northern Barbarians* (Oxford: Clarendon Press, 1987)

Tomlin, R.S.O. 'The late Roman Empire', in General Sir John Hackett (ed.) *Warfare in the Ancient World*, pp. 222–49 (London: Guild Publishing, 1989)

Trevelyan, G.M. *Garibaldi's Defence of the Roman Republic* (London: Longmans, Green, & Co., 1907)

Ward-Perkins, J.B. *From Classical Antiquity to the Middle Ages: Urban Public Building in Northern and Central Italy, AD 300–850* (Oxford: Clarendon Press, 1984)

Watson, A. *Aurelian and the Third Century* (London: Routledge, 1999, 2004)

Williams, S. *Diocletian and the Roman Recovery* (London: Routledge, 1985, 2000)

Wolfram, H. *History of the Goths* (Berkeley: University of California Press, 1988)

INDEX

References to illustrations are shown in **bold**.